Overcoming Eating Disorders

✓ **Treatments** *That Work*™

Overcoming Eating Disorders

A COGNITIVE-BEHAVIORAL THERAPY APPROACH FOR BULIMIA NERVOSA AND BINGE-EATING DISORDER

SECOND EDITION

Therapist Guide

W. Stewart Agras • Robin F. Apple

OXFORD
UNIVERSITY PRESS

2008

OXFORD
UNIVERSITY PRESS

Oxford University Press, Inc., publishes works that further
Oxford University's objective of excellence
in research, scholarship, and education.

Oxford   New York
Auckland   Cape Town   Dar es Salaam   Hong Kong   Karachi
Kuala Lumpur   Madrid   Melbourne   Mexico City   Nairobi
New Delhi   Shanghai   Taipei   Toronto

With offices in
Argentina   Austria   Brazil   Chile   Czech Republic   France   Greece
Guatemala   Hungary   Italy   Japan   Poland   Portugal   Singapore
South Korea   Switzerland   Thailand   Turkey   Ukraine   Vietnam

Copyright © 2008 by Oxford University Press, Inc.

Published by Oxford University Press, Inc.
198 Madison Avenue, New York, New York 10016

www.oup.com

Oxford is a registered trademark of Oxford University Press

Library of Congress Cataloging-in-Publication Data
Agras, W. Stewart.
Overcoming eating disorders : a cognitive-behavioral therapy approach for
bulimia nervosa and binge-eating disorder / Stewart Agras and Robin F. Apple.—2nd ed.
p. cm. — (Treatments that work)
Includes bibliographical references.
ISBN 978-0-19-531169-3
1. Bulimia—Treatment. 2. Compulsive eating—Treatment. 3. Cognitive therapy.
I. Apple, Robin F. (Robin Faye) II. Title. III. Series: Treatments that work.
[DNLM: 1. Bulimia Nervosa—therapy. 2. Cognitive Therapy—methods.
WM 175 A2770 2008]
RC552.B84A37 2008
616.85′263—dc22   2007012365

9   8   7   6   5   4   3   2   1

Printed in the United States of America
on acid-free paper

About Treatments *ThatWork*™

Stunning developments in healthcare have taken place over the last several years, but many of our widely accepted interventions and strategies in mental health and behavioral medicine have been brought into question by research evidence as not only lacking benefit, but perhaps, inducing harm. Other strategies have been proven effective using the best current standards of evidence, resulting in broad-based recommendations to make these practices more available to the public. Several recent developments are behind this revolution. First, we have arrived at a much deeper understanding of pathology, both psychological and physical, which has led to the development of new, more precisely targeted interventions. Second, our research methodologies have improved substantially, such that we have reduced threats to internal and external validity, making the outcomes more directly applicable to clinical situations. Third, governments around the world and healthcare systems and policymakers have decided that the quality of care should improve, that it should be evidence based, and that it is in the public's interest to ensure that this happens (Barlow, 2004; Institute of Medicine, 2001).

Of course, the major stumbling block for clinicians everywhere is the accessibility of newly developed evidence-based psychological interventions. Workshops and books can go only so far in acquainting responsible and conscientious practitioners with the latest behavioral healthcare practices and their applicability to individual patients. This new series, Treatments *ThatWork*™, is devoted to communicating these exciting new interventions to clinicians on the frontlines of practice.

The manuals and workbooks in this series contain step-by-step detailed procedures for assessing and treating specific problems and diagnoses. But this series goes beyond the books and manuals by providing ancillary materials to approximate the supervisory process and assist practitioners in implementing these procedures in their practice.

In our emerging healthcare system, the growing consensus is that evidence-based practice offers the most responsible course of action for the mental health professional. All behavioral healthcare clinicians deeply desire to provide the best possible care for their patients. In this series, our aim is to close the dissemination and information gap and make that possible.

The *Overcoming Eating Disorders, Second Edition* program addresses the cognitive-behavioral treatment of bulimia nervosa and binge-eating disorder. Approximately 5–10% of girls and women in the United States suffer from eating disorders, and another 15% have some kind of disordered eating patterns. CBT has been proven the most effective treatment for helping these individuals improve their eating habits and overcome bulimia and binge-eating disorder. Over the course of this program, patients will learn to regularize their eating habits, identify their triggers for bingeing episodes, replace bingeing episodes with more-pleasurable activities, and maintain the gains they make during treatment. This revised therapist guide includes expanded information regarding weight and shape concerns and an entirely new chapter on adapting the treatment for use as a time-limited, therapist-assisted self-help program. Complete with step-by-step instructions for delivering the treatment, this guide is an indispensable resource that no clinician can do without.

David H. Barlow, Editor-in-Chief,
Treatments *That Work*™
Boston, Massachusetts

Contents

Treatment Phase 3: Maintaining Change

Guided Self-Help

Information About Bulimia Nervosa and Binge-Eating Disorder and This Treatment Program

Chapter 1   *Introductory Information for Therapists*

Background Information and Purpose of This Program

This therapist guide contains background information essential to the understanding of bulimia nervosa and binge-eating disorder and their treatment with cognitive-behavioral therapy (CBT) and guided self-help based on the principles of CBT. It is intended for use by qualified therapists who have had some experience in the assessment and treatment of eating disorders. It is also useful for the therapist in training, when it should be used under the guidance of a therapist who has experience using the manual. It provides guidance regarding the details of specific therapy sessions and phases of therapy, and it is therefore essential that it be read before conducting therapy. Moreover, to avoid therapist drift, we advise all therapists to review the guide from time to time. The accompanying patient workbook, *Overcoming Your Eating Disorder*, should also be read by the therapist because it contains information linked to specific treatment sessions and procedures. There is an additional workbook for patients who wish to participate in the shorter, therapist-assisted self-help program outlined in Chapter 16. More-detailed information about this workbook can be found in the same chapter.

The treatment program described may be conducted either in the context of individual or group therapy, with the necessary adjustments dictated by the form of therapy.

The Nature of Bulimia Nervosa and Binge-Eating Disorder

Studies of bulimia nervosa (BN) and binge-eating disorder (BED) find that these disorders tend to run in families, suggesting either genetic transmission or shared psychological factors affecting family members.

Twin studies suggest that bulimia nervosa is heritable, accounting for perhaps half the variance in causation, although the nature of what is inherited is unknown. Studies suggest that brain serotonin levels may be lower than normal in the bulimic, and that the high carbohydrate intake tends to alleviate that deficit. Low serotonin levels may also be associated with depression, a frequent accompaniment of bulimia.

Environmental risk factors are also important in the causation of bulimia. The pressure on women to achieve a thin body has increased in the last 25 years, preceding and later accompanying the sudden rise in the number of cases of bulimia nervosa presenting to clinics across the Western world in the early '70s. This trend appears to result from a portrayal of thinner ideal body types in the media combined with a proliferation of articles describing various types of diets. This trend leads many women to adopt a thin ideal. Paradoxically, overweight and obesity are increasing and simultaneously making it more difficult to achieve the thin ideal. Risk factors predisposing one to bulimia nervosa include being teased about weight and shape by peers and parents and having dietary restriction and weight-control practices imposed by parents. Social pressure to be thin appears to be a causal risk factor for bulimic symptoms. Parental or childhood overweight is also a risk factor for bulimia, although recent work suggests that it is parental eating-disorder psychopathology in the presence of overweight that is the risk factor. Negative affect is also a risk factor for eating psychopathology. It should be noted that sexual or physical abuse are often associated with bulimia nervosa but are not specific risk factors for the disorder. In general, it appears that psychological influences within the family are specific to particular individuals and are not shared by all children within the family, with gender being an important factor in how such influences work. Although risk factors are important in the prevention of eating disorders, factors that maintain the disorder are more important in treatment.

Binge eating, common to both bulimia nervosa and binge-eating disorder, is characterized by a sense of loss of control over eating. This sense of losing control and being unable to stop eating may be associated with changes in mood and conflicting thoughts about food. Negative transient moods of anxiety, anger, or depression that trigger a binge often result from unsatisfactory interpersonal interactions. There may be an overwhelming urge to eat, accompanied by positive feelings sometimes described as a thrill or as excitement, or negative feelings such as anxiety, anger, guilt, depression, or boredom. Sometimes the binge is a rebellion against perceived restraint by others. The cognitive components may consist of thoughts such as "I don't want to do this, I shouldn't be eating like this" or "I'm being a pig again," or positive thoughts such as "I really deserve a treat, so I should eat the ice cream."

Binges may be large or small; in the bulimic, they average about 1,500 calories, and in those with binge-eating disorder about 1,000 calories, ranging in both disorders from 100 to 7,000 or more calories—approximately the amount of food that might be eaten in two or more meals. Large, or objective, binges, are differentiated from small, or subjective, binges. For example, the diagnostic manual of the American Psychiatric Association (*DSM–IV–TR*) requires that binges consist of eating a large amount of food. Whether or not the size of the binge matters is still unknown. However, subjective binges may be as upsetting to the patient as objective binges. Some evidence suggests that objective binges are the first to disappear during treatment. However, the assessment of subjective binges is difficult because it depends on assessing loss of control. Studies have found excellent agreement between two ratings for objective binges but poor agreement for subjective binges.

The foods eaten in binges vary widely but typically consist of sweet (often high-fat), easily swallowed foods, such as ice cream, cookies, breads, cereals, pasta, and so on. Some patients, however, binge on several servings of a main course. Patients with bulimia nervosa often drink large quantities of fluids to facilitate self-induced vomiting. The most commonly reported trigger for a binge is a transient negative mood, followed in frequency by dietary restriction and feelings of hunger and/or deprivation. In bulimia nervosa, purging follows binge eating, most usually taking the form of self-induced vomiting and/or use of laxatives; diuretics are less often abused. Less commonly, bulimics will chew binge food and then spit it out. Excessive exercise, aimed at controlling weight and shape is also common in bulimia nervosa, whereas fasting for more than 24 hours is relatively uncommon.

The average reported age for the onset of binge eating in both bulimia nervosa and binge-eating disorder is 19 years, usually followed a few months later by purging in bulimia nervosa, and by gradual weight gain in binge-eating disorder. However, about 10% of patients with bulimia nervosa are overweight, whereas some 25–30% of patients have a past history of anorexia nervosa. About 10% of patients with binge-eating disorder have purged in the past, sometimes meeting criteria for bulimia nervosa at that time. Others have tried to purge but find that they cannot do it or that it is repulsive to them. Both bulimia nervosa and binge-eating disorder are frequently accompanied by other psychological problems that may need to be treated separately from the eating disorder. The problems most frequently associated with eating disorders are depression; anxiety disorders, including panic disorder and social phobia; personality disorders, especially disorders associated with emotional instability and impulsive behaviors; and alcohol or drug abuse. Hence, it is necessary to make a thorough assessment of comorbid psychopathology before beginning treatment for the eating disorder.

Diagnostic Criteria for Bulimia Nervosa

In the following outline we list the *DSM–IV–TR* criteria for bulimia nervosa.

A. Recurrent episodes of binge eating.

An episode of binge eating is characterized by both of the following:
(1) eating, in a discrete period of time (e.g., within any 2-hour period), an amount of food that is definitely larger than most people would eat during a similar period of time and under similar circumstances
(2) a sense of lack of control over eating during the episode (e.g., a feeling that one cannot stop eating or control what or how much one is eating)

B. Recurrent inappropriate compensatory behavior in order to prevent weight gain, such as self-induced vomiting; misuse of laxatives, diuretics, enemas, or other medications; fasting; or excessive exercise.

C. The binge eating and inappropriate compensatory behaviors both occur, on average, at least twice a week for 3 months.

D.   Self-evaluation is unduly influenced by body shape and weight.

E.   The disturbance does not occur exclusively during episodes of anorexia nervosa.

Specify type:

Purging Type. During the current episode of bulimia nervosa, the person has regularly engaged in self-induced vomiting or the misuse of laxatives, diuretics, or enemas.

Nonpurging Type. During the current episode of bulimia nervosa, the person has used other inappropriate compensatory behaviors, such as fasting or excessive exercise, but has not regularly engaged in self-induced vomiting or the misuse of laxatives, diuretics, or enemas.

Diagnostic Criteria for Binge-Eating Disorder

In the following outline, we list the *DSM–IV–TR* criteria for binge-eating disorder.

A.   Recurrent episodes of binge eating.

An episode of binge eating is characterized by both of the following:
(1)   eating, in a discrete period of time (e.g., within any 2-hour period), an amount of food that is definitely larger than most people would eat in a similar period of time under similar circumstances
(2)   a sense of lack of control over eating during the episode (e.g., a feeling that one cannot stop eating or control what or how much one is eating)

B.   The binge-eating episodes are associated with three (or more) of the following:
(1)   eating much more rapidly than normal
(2)   eating until feeling uncomfortably full
(3)   eating large amounts of food when not feeling physically hungry

(4) eating alone because of being embarrassed by how much one is eating

(5) feeling disgusted with oneself, depressed, or very guilty after overeating

C. Marked distress regarding binge eating is present.

D. The binge eating occurs, on average, at least 2 days a week for 6 months.

E. The binge eating is not associated with the regular use of inappropriate compensatory behaviors (e.g., purging, fasting, excessive exercise) and does not occur exclusively during the course of anorexia nervosa or bulimia nervosa.

Patients who do not meet the full criteria for bulimia nervosa or binge-eating disorder, for example, they binge eat less frequently than twice a week or do not experience large binges, are classified as having eating disorder not otherwise specified (EDNOS). Most studies have found few differences between the subclinical variants of BN and BED and the full syndrome. It may be that most cases of EDNOS are either beginning cases that may worsen to the full syndrome, or full-syndrome cases that are improving. In any event, many patients with EDNOS may benefit from treatment.

Development of This Treatment Program and Evidence Base

The therapist guide and corresponding patient workbook derive from several years of conducting controlled clinical trials of the treatment of bulimia nervosa and binge-eating disorder at Stanford University. Manuals were produced for each of these trials, with each revision resting on the experience of conducting therapy in controlled trials and treating patients in our Eating Disorders Clinic. Further development derives from collaborative work with colleagues, including Christopher Fairburn at Oxford University, Katherine Halmi at Cornell University, James Mitchell at the University of North Dakota, Denise Wilfley at the University of Washington–St. Louis, and Terence Wilson at Rutgers University, among others. In addition, the clinical and research literature on bulimia nervosa and binge-eating disorder has led to further refinements of the guided self-help (GSH) treatment approach discussed in Chapter 16.

Cognitive-behavioral therapy has been found to be the most effective psychotherapeutic approach to the treatment of bulimia nervosa in the short-term and is usually recommended as the first-line therapy for bulimia nervosa. CBT has been found more effective than other treatments, including waiting-list control conditions, non-directive therapy, pill placebo, manualized psychodynamic therapy (supportive-expressive therapy), stress management, and antidepressant treatment, in reducing binge eating and purging. Some 50–60% of patients with BN who complete a course of CBT remit, while another 20% are much improved. Between one quarter and one third of bulimic patients are abstinent at the end of treatment with intent-to-treat analyses. This is because 20–25% of participants drop out of treatment. At follow-up after 1 to 5 years, there is reasonably good maintenance of improvement. In the longest follow-up study to date, Fairburn and his colleagues at Oxford University followed bulimic patients treated with cognitive-behavioral therapy for five years post treatment. Nearly 60% had no eating disorder, and a further 20% now had a subclinical disorder (EDNOS). The remainder had not remitted, with a small percentage diagnosed as having anorexia nervosa. Hence, relapse rates for the successfully treated patient are low, and the benefits of treatment are long lasting. In addition to the improvements in binge eating and purging, there are usually significant reductions in depression and often improvements in social functioning. Dropout rates, as noted, average about 25%. Factors associated with dropout include: relative youth of patients, having comorbid conditions such as personality disorders and impulsivity, and having comorbid depression. However, various studies have found various predictors of dropout, and no study has been particularly clinically useful in predicting who is going to drop out. Studies have also described several nonspecific predictors of poor outcome, including low self-esteem, low weight or previous anorexia nervosa, a higher frequency or severity of binge eating, comorbid personality disorder, and depression. As with the predictors of dropout, none of these factors is clinically useful in predicting who will do poorly with treatment. However, larger scale studies have shown that early response to CBT, in terms of reducing vomiting, usefully predicts outcome both at the end of treatment and at follow-up: those who have reduced the frequency of their purging episodes by less than 70% by Session 6 (Week 4 of treatment) are more likely to be treatment non-responders. The sensitivity of this test was 86%, with a specificity of 69%. Using these criteria to select patients likely to fail CBT and to add a second treatment, 74% would get the correct treatment; 4% of those who would have recovered with CBT would get the second treatment unnecessarily; and 22% who were assigned to CBT would fail that treatment. The clinical implication of this finding is that in patients who do not meet the cutoff after 4 weeks (6 sessions) of treatment, the reasons for a slow response should be reviewed and remedial action taken.

It will often be the case that such individuals have not sufficiently altered their eating pattern. For example, one study found that a pattern of eating that had at least 80 meals combined with at least 21 afternoon snacks within a 28-day period was associated with an abstinence rate of 70%. In contrast, for subjects having between 72 and 80 meals, those having more than 11 evening snacks have an abstinence rate of 4%. The importance of the afternoon snack was particularly noteworthy, with those having at least 80 meals but fewer afternoon snacks having an abstinence rate of 23%. This makes excellent clinical sense because the gap between lunch and dinner is usually the longest in a person's day, and hunger is more likely to be intense by the evening; hence, the tendency to binge eat is greater if one forgoes the afternoon snack. There may be other reasons underlying a slow response to CBT, for example, depression, disorganization, a relationship problem, and so on. These problems may have to be addressed before treating the eating disorder in order to free the patient to make appropriate changes in his or her eating behavior.

Many patients fear that altering their eating patterns will lead to weight gain. However, in most studies, individuals with bulimia nervosa treated with CBT gain little weight; hence, patients can be reassured that weight gains are unlikely. Clinical experience suggests that the overweight patient with bulimia nervosa tends to lose a little weight, whereas the underweight patient who has often suffered from anorexia nervosa in the past may have to gain some weight in order to improve. This is often difficult for those low-weight bulimics with past anorexia nervosa, presumably accounting for the poorer results with this group of individuals. Depressive symptoms also show improvement with CBT.

Studies of the mechanism underlying the effectiveness of CBT have found that lowering dietary restraint early in treatment mediates the outcome of treatment. This confirms the hypothesis that dietary restraint is an important factor in maintaining binge eating.

The only psychotherapeutic treatment that may be as effective as CBT for the treatment of bulimia nervosa is interpersonal psychotherapy (IPT). A recent multisite study involving 220 participants found that CBT was significantly superior to IPT in the number of patients with BN recovered at the end of treatment, although by 8–12 months follow-up, the outcomes for the two treatments were not distinguishable. Hence, IPT, because it is slower to exert its effects, should be regarded as a second-line treatment for BN.

Other forms of treatment, such as dialectical behavior therapy, have not been studied sufficiently at this point to reveal how useful they may be in the treatment of bulimia nervosa. It is also clear, however, that the percentage of abstinent individuals at the end of treatment with CBT, while higher than that with other existing treatments, is by no means ideal. Hence, it continues to be important to improve CBT. At this point, there are no firm data on methods to improve treatment. One suggestion is to treat those with current major depression, usually about 20% of those seeking treatment, for their depression before beginning treatment for their bulimic symptoms. Fairburn has also suggested using a more modular approach to treatment, attempting to match treatment modules to patient needs. This can be achieved with this manual by focusing on the specific factors that trigger binge eating for a particular patient after progress has been made to establish a more normal eating pattern.

The controlled psychological-treatment studies in binge-eating disorder suggest that CBT and interpersonal psychotherapy are equally effective. Recovery rates are somewhat better than for the treatment of BN, with about 60% recovering at the end of treatment in intent-to-treat analyses, compared with 20–35% for BN. As is the case for BN, treatment effects are well maintained. However, unlike for bulimia nervosa, IPT appears to act as rapidly as CBT in the treatment of binge-eating disorder; therefore, it is reasonable to use either of these therapies initially in the treatment of BED. Unfortunately, it appears that adding interpersonal therapy for those who do not respond to CBT is not useful: No patient who failed to improve with CBT improved with IPT. In a one-

year follow-up study of patients treated with CBT followed by a modi-
fied form of weight-loss treatment, patients who continued to abstain
from binge eating lost about 14 lbs, whereas those who did not stop
binge eating gained about 7 lbs. Hence, it appears that stopping binge
eating is associated with weight loss. Most recently, initial studies suggest
that dialectical behavior therapy may be useful in the treatment of BED,
with recovery rates similar to those with CBT or IPT. However, there are
indications that relapse occurs in a substantial proportion of individuals
within a few months following the end of treatment.

There is, at present, some controversy about whether weight-loss therapy
alone may be as effective as CBT in treating binge-eating disorder. Most
of the studies that bear on this issue have major methodological problems. However, one study recently reported a comparison of therapist-
assisted guided self-help based on CBT with weight-loss treatment and
a control condition. In intent-to-treat analyses, GSH was more effective
in reducing binge eating (46% abstinent) than was either the weight-loss
condition (18%) or a control condition that focused on self-monitoring
(13%). Unfortunately, weight loss was minimal and identical across
treatments; therefore, it is possible that the specific effect of weight-loss
treatment was absent in this study.

In general, the research findings regarding the treatment of bulimia nervosa and binge-eating disorder suggest that although several types of
therapy may be useful in the treatment of these disorders, cognitive-
behavioral therapy can be considered the treatment of choice both for
bulimia nervosa and for binge-eating disorder, although interpersonal
therapy is as effective as CBT for binge-eating disorder but slower to
exert its effects in bulimia nervosa.

Alternative Treatments

Psychopharmacological Treatment for Bulimia Nervosa

The use of antidepressants in BN was sparked by the observation that
depression is frequently a comorbid feature of the disorder. Eating dis-
turbances frequently accompany depression, suggesting a link between
the two disorders. However, it is now known that degree of depression

is not associated with the outcome of antidepressant treatment of bulimia nervosa. In 1982, two groups of researchers conducted small-scale uncontrolled studies suggesting that both monoamine oxidase inhibitors (MAOIs) and tricyclic antidepressants (TCAs) reduced binge eating and purging. These observations were followed by a series of double-blind placebo-controlled studies confirming the utility of antidepressants in treating patients with BN, at least in the short term. Many antidepressant agents have been found effective, including imipramine, desipramine, phenelzine, bromofarin, trazodone, bupropion, fluoxetine, and other selective serotonin reuptake inhibitors (SSRIs). In these studies, the median remission rate was 32%, and the median dropout rate was 23%. Put another way, of 100 patients with BN, some 77 will persevere with a course of medication treatment, and 25 will be in remission at the end of treatment with a single antidepressant. Walsh and his colleagues found that there is a rapid response to desipramine in terms of reduction of bulimic symptoms. They concluded that non-responders to medication could be identified after 2 weeks of treatment.

Antidepressants are prescribed in the same dosage used for treating depression with the exception of fluoxetine, for which it was found that a dosage of 60 mg daily is more effective than one of 20 mg daily in reducing binge eating and purging in a placebo-controlled trial involving 387 bulimic women. One problem with medication that is given at times other than bedtime is that a significant amount of medication may be purged through subsequent vomiting. Side effects and reasons for dropout from the various medications are similar to those observed in the treatment of depression, with the exception of bupropion, for which a higher than expected proportion of patients with BN had a grand mal seizure. The authors concluded that bupropion should not be used in BN until the reason for the high proportion of seizures in these patients is established. Additionally, because of the dietary restrictions associated with the use of monoamine oxidase inhibitors, to which the impulsive bulimic may not adhere, and the availability of a wide range of other effective antidepressants, MAOI's should probably not be used to treat BN. A recent study found that fluvoxamine (an SSRI) was no more effective than a placebo in a large-scale placebo-controlled study. Moreover, three participants suffered grand mal seizures and five developed abnormal liver function. The authors concluded that fluvoxamine should not be used to treat bulimia nervosa.

Overall, it appears that most antidepressants are effective in the treatment of BN in the short term; however, less is known about long-term effectiveness. A substantial fraction of individuals relapse in the first few months of treatment, although some of these will respond to a different antidepressant. The optimal length of treatment has not been well established. One controlled study compared 16 weeks of desipramine for the treatment of bulimia nervosa with 24 weeks of treatment with desipramine. Those who were withdrawn from medication after 16 weeks of treatment relapsed to pretreatment levels of bulimic symptoms, whereas those who were withdrawn after 24 weeks maintained their gains both at the end of treatment and at 1-year follow-up. Many clinicians, however, maintain their bulimic patients on medication for up to 1 year.

Combining Medication and Psychotherapy to Treat Bulimia Nervosa

The existence of two different and effective treatments, antidepressant medication and cognitive-behavioral therapy, leads to the question of whether the combination of such treatments would be more effective than either one alone. Several controlled trials have examined this question. Overall, the benefits of adding medication to CBT on bulimic symptoms are small, although there are clear benefits in reducing depression.

Medication Following Failure of Psychotherapy

One controlled study examined whether fluoxetine at a dosage of 60 mg was helpful for patients with bulimia nervosa for whom a course of either cognitive-behavioral or interpersonal therapy had been unsuccessful. In this placebo-controlled trial, fluoxetine was significantly superior to placebo for these patients, suggesting that antidepressant medication may be useful to those for whom psychotherapy is unsuccessful.

Other Medications

Because opioids are involved in the control of eating, there has been some interest in using opiate antagonists in eating disorders. One study involving 16 women with bulimia nervosa compared low (50–100 mg/day) and high (200–300 mg/day) doses of naltrexone, finding that high-dosage patients with BN fared best in reducing their binge eating and purging. However, this was a short-term study, and no data on full recovery were given. Additionally, one patient in the high-dose group demonstrated elevations in liver-function tests, but these normalized after the dose was reduced. The authors suggest that liver function should be monitored frequently when using high-dose naltrexone. A further study found daily administration of 100 mg of naltrexone no more effective than placebos in reducing the frequency of binge eating and purging in bulimia nervosa, although the duration of binges was reduced significantly. Topiramate has also been used in the treatment of bulimia nervosa, producing modest improvements in binge eating and purging. Further studies of topiramate are needed at this point.

Comprehensive Treatment of Bulimia Nervosa

For the most part, patients with BN are best treated as outpatients, unless there are either medical or psychiatric reasons for hospitalization (e.g., an intercurrent physical illness or comorbid psychopathology requiring hospitalization, such as a major depression with suicidality). One reason for the usefulness of outpatient treatment is that gains made in the hospital may not carry over to the patient's home, where there are more-complex food stimuli and greater stress.

At this time, no clear guidelines exist regarding the sequencing of pharmacological and psychological therapies. Given the superiority of CBT to medication, psychological treatment should be regarded as the best initial approach, with medication being added if the response to CBT is unsatisfactory. On the other hand, antidepressant medication is a simpler, less expensive treatment and is more widely available than is CBT. Patients should be told of these findings so that they can make an informed choice. In cases where there is marked depression accompanying the bulimic symptoms, antidepressant therapy should be used to alleviate the depressive symptoms before beginning CBT. If the bulimic symptoms are not controlled, then CBT should be added.

Psychopharmacological Treatment for Binge-Eating Disorder

For the most part, double-blind placebo-controlled studies of the use of antidepressants in BED have shown that active medication reduces binge eating significantly more than do placebos. In the largest pharmacological study to date, fluvoxamine at an average dosage of 260 mg was compared with placebo in a 9-week multisite study involving 85 participants meeting *DSM* criteria for BED. Binge eating decreased significantly more in the medication group than in the placebo group. Other studies, however, have not found a significant effect of medication, citing large placebo effects. Nonetheless, antidepressants appear useful in the treatment of BED, although the effects appear smaller than those attributable to CBT. One study found that CBT was superior to fluoxetine in reducing binge eating. However, in that study, fluoxetine was not superior to placebo.

More recently, there has been considerable interest in the use of antiepileptic drugs, which appear to lead to decrements in both binge eating and weight. A controlled study using topiramate found that 64% of the topiramate group and 30% of the placebo group had remitted by the end of treatment. The mean weight loss in the topiramate group was 5.9 kg, compared to 1.2 kg in the placebo group. Open-label studies suggest that similar antiepileptic medications have a similar effect on binge eating and weight. Given the effects on weight, these medications may eventually find a significant place in the treatment of binge-eating disorder.

Comprehensive Treatment of Binge-Eating Disorder

Binge-eating disorder presents a problem for treatment because of the accompanying overweight or obesity in most cases. It is important for patients to understand that CBT is not associated with significant weight losses and that attempts to diet may be associated with a relapse of binge eating. It is probably important to incorporate a move toward a healthy diet and a mild exercise program into CBT, so that weight can be kept in under control. As was the case in the treatment of BN, those with current major depression should be treated with antidepressants before beginning CBT. There is little information on sequencing treatments for BED, although one study found that adding desipramine to CBT, followed by weight-loss treatment, significantly enhanced weight loss. Such weight losses might be even greater with the use of anti-epileptic medication such as topiramate, although there have been no studies that bear on this point.

Guided Self-Help for Bulimia Nervosa and Binge-Eating Disorder

Self-help manuals with or without therapist supervision have recently gained in popularity for the treatment of a number of psychological disorders, including bulimia nervosa and binge-eating disorder. Self-help manuals based on CBT educate patients about the restraint model and offer guidance in the form of interventions like those that a therapist would present during CBT. Such interventions include educating the patient about the nature of bulimia, presenting the CBT model of bulimia, introducing the use of self-monitoring, prescribing new eating patterns, and teaching the patient exercises to challenge distorted cognitions and attitudes toward weight and shape. Self-help manuals are most effective when combined with several brief therapy sessions aimed at evaluating progress and dealing with any stumbling blocks the patient might encounter. The number and duration of sessions have varied, as have the type and level of skill of the therapist. At this point it seems that master's-level therapists can conduct this treatment successfully, and that 8–10 sessions of 25 minutes each suffice for guidance. The setting may also matter; studies have found little benefit for guided self-help conducted in a medical outpatient or family practice setting, whereas studies in other settings, such as specialty clinics, have had greater success. In GSH, the therapist refers the patient back to the book to answer questions about therapy, thus enhancing the importance of the book and encouraging the patient to read it. A bulimic patient's significant others might also be interested in reading to enhance their understanding of and ability to cope with their loved one's eating disorder.

The amount of controlled research examining the efficacy of self-help manuals for the treatment of bulimia has been steadily increasing over the past few years. The most useful comparison is between GSH and CBT. Several moderate-sized studies suggest that GSH is equivalent in effectiveness to full-scale CBT. One 4-year follow-up of patients with bulimia nervosa treated with GSH, although small, suggested that there was good maintenance of improvement. A recent large-scale multisite study, in which 147 individuals with bulimia nervosa were randomly allocated to CBT and 146 to GSH, found no difference between the two groups either at the end of treatment or at 1-year follow-up. Interestingly, those with poorer social adjustment and more eating-disorder psychopathology did better with GSH, whereas those with good social adjustment and less severe eating-disorder psychopathology did better with CBT. It may be that those with poorer social adjustment have fewer resources and cannot spare the time or effort involved in full-scale CBT. GSH was significantly less costly per remitted patient. Hence, there is a good deal of evidence for the effectiveness of GSH in treating bulimia nervosa.

As is the case for bulimia nervosa, there are now several studies that suggest that GSH is as effective as CBT in the treatment of BED. In a large-scale multisite study, GSH was shown to be as effective as IPT in reducing binge eating at 12 months after treatment. Hence, there is growing evidence to suggest that GSH is an effective approach to the treatment of BED.

Outline of This Treatment Program

The cognitive-behavioral model of bulimia nervosa is shown in Figure 1.1. One of the key maintaining features of the disorder is dietary restriction, which in turn leads to weight loss, hunger, disinhibition of eating, and finally, binge eating. In bulimia nervosa, the threat of weight gain eventually leads to purging. Dieting in both the bulimic and the binge eater often follows a period of actual or perceived weight gain. It seems likely that young women with low self-esteem are more likely to become overly concerned about their weight and shape, perhaps restricting food intake to a greater extent than do their peers. Binge eating is followed by purging in the bulimic; in both bulimia nervosa and binge-eating disorder, guilt follows the binge (and purge), with a consequent lowering of self-esteem. Cognitive influences are found in rules about, and perceptions of, weight and shape; rules about what foods to eat or to avoid; rules about amounts of food to eat; and often-faulty perceptions of having eaten too much when the amount is within the normal range. Distortions about weight and shape are also common. Negative mood stemming from negative interpersonal interactions also leads to binge eating. Indeed, studies suggest that 70% of binge episodes are triggered by a transient negative mood.

As can be seen in Figure 1.1, a vicious cycle leads from dietary restriction to binge eating (and purging) and back to dietary restriction. Negative affect predisposes one to binge eating, particularly in the presence of dietary restriction.

Each of the levels shown in Figure 1.1 is associated with particular cognitions. For example, at the level of self-esteem may be a deep cognitive appraisal "I'm no good"; at the level of weight and shape concerns, there may be the perception "If I gain any more weight, no one will like me." Cognitive-behavioral therapy is aimed first at reducing restrained eating,

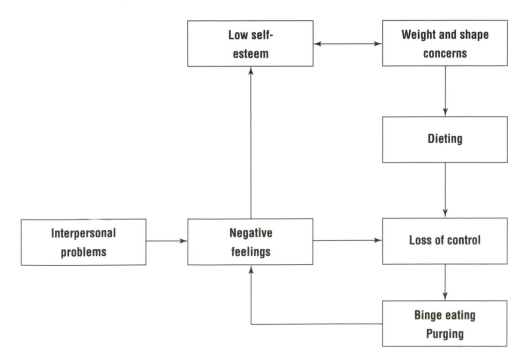

Figure 1.1
A Model of Factors Maintaining Binge Eating and Purging

and second, at dealing with other factors maintaining binge eating. These factors include weight and shape concerns, faulty thinking regarding eating, and triggers of binge eating, such as negative affect stemming from faulty interpersonal interactions. The full CBT treatment program is intended to take approximately 18–20 sessions spread over 6 months. Individual sessions are usually 50 minutes long; group sessions are usually 90 minutes long.

Treatment is divided into three overlapping phases. The length of each phase and the degree of overlap of phases is determined by each patient's needs and progress. It is assumed that the therapist will make a thorough assessment of the patient's problem and of any comorbid psychopathology before beginning treatment. In addition, it is important to examine the pros and cons of treatment with the patient, particularly examining any ambivalence to treatment and resolving these issues with a form of motivational interviewing as detailed in Chapter 3. This is important because we know that patients who make significant changes in the first few sessions of treatment are those who will do well in treatment. It is important that potential patients understand this and can give treatment sufficient priority. This means a willingness to take risks and, in particular, to rapidly regularize their meal patterns so that no more than 3–4 hours elapses between eating episodes.

The key principles and procedures involved in using CBT for bulimia nervosa and binge eating are:

1. The patient must establish a pattern of regular eating that consists of three meals and two snacks a day, with no more than 3–4 hours between eating episodes. It is important to establish this pattern early in treatment. This pattern allows the reestablishment of hunger and satiety signals that have been disrupted by excessive dieting. To establish this pattern, it is necessary to explain the CBT model to the patient, demonstrating the personal applicability of the model, and also to introduce relevant educational points.

2. Once the pattern has become more or less established, other forms of dieting are tackled, for example, introducing more food and eventually feared foods.

616.85

AGR

3. Therapy then investigates and deals with the various circumstances and thoughts that trigger binge eating.

4. Finally, a relapse-prevention plan is formed.

It is important to maintain a steady focus on these procedures and not to digress into irrelevant materials.

Phase 1: Behavior Change

Although not mandatory, it has been found that completing the first four sessions within 2 weeks helps get treatment off to a rapid start and facilitates the development of a satisfactory working relationship between patient and therapist. The goal of Phase 1 is to present an individualized model of bulimia nervosa to the patient. The main elements of the model are that dieting to lose weight (usually quite obvious from the patient's history of weight loss before beginning to binge) leads to excessive hunger, which eventually leads to loss of control over eating and to binge eating. For the patient with bulimia nervosa, this leads to purging and to guilt, with subsequent lowering of self-esteem. It is this behavior pattern, together with the extreme weight and shape concerns that these patients exhibit, that maintains the disorder. On average, those with bulimia nervosa will have lost about 20 lbs in the period during which they began to binge eat. However, it should be noted that most individuals with BN who present for treatment are no longer losing weight and hence are in caloric balance.

It is important to teach patients to use self-monitoring to clarify the details of their eating habits, using these data to understand the details of the patients' dieting and to monitor progress in establishing regular eating. For the patient with binge-eating disorder, the excess calories consumed while binge eating lead to inexorable weight gain, leading in turn to increased concern about weight and shape, and to guilt about gaining weight. To overcome this pattern of eating, that is, alternating dietary restriction and binge eating, the patient is encouraged to eat three meals and two snacks each day at regular intervals (by the clock), as for the treatment of bulimia nervosa. Formal problem solving may be introduced in this phase to help the patient overcome specific problems; toward the end of this phase, work begins on consuming a broader array of foods. By the end of this phase, which usually lasts between six and eight sessions, the patient should be eating regularly, with only occasional lapses, which, by reducing dietary restriction, should greatly lower the frequency of binge eating (and purging).

The main focus of Phase 1 is to establish a pattern of regular eating using a personalized CBT model as a rationale and, as needed, using educational information about dieting and purging.

Phase 2: Identifying Binge Triggers

The general aims of Phase 1 continue to be implemented in the second and longest phase of treatment, but in Phase 2, the focus shifts to alleviating other binge-eating triggers. These strategies include further reducing dietary restraint by broadening food choices to decrease the number of feared and avoided foods; altering distorted perceptions of shape and weight and reducing concerns about weight and shape by using behavioral tasks such as observing the shape and weight of other women; and reducing compulsive behaviors such as frequently checking "fat" areas of the body, frequently looking in mirrors, and so on. In addition, interpersonal binge-eating triggers, which are often associated with transient negative moods, may need to be addressed. Finally, cognitive restructuring concerning rigid food rules and other distorted beliefs about food is often useful.

Phase 3: Relapse Prevention

The last three sessions of treatment are usually devoted in part to reviewing the positive changes that have occurred during treatment as a result of the patient's behavior changes. In addition, residual problems are defined, and the patient is encouraged to look ahead and to delineate a plan to handle these problems to avoid lapses. At least some of these problems will already have been dealt with in the second phase of treatment. To allow more time for such residual problems to surface, it is suggested that the final three sessions be held at 2-week intervals.

Session Structure

Therapy proceeds more smoothly when the session is well structured. Hence, each session should be structured as follows. After greeting the patient and making a general inquiry as to how things are going, you should review with the patient the homework assigned at the end of the last session, including the self-monitoring records completed since the last session. Depending on the record review and the phase and progress of therapy, the therapist should then set a specific agenda for the session. This should form the main work for the session and should be followed by a review of the main points covered, which should naturally lead to assigning specific homework to be done before the next session.

Using the Workbook

The corresponding workbook is intended for the bulimic or binge-eating patient to use in conjunction with this treatment program and under the supervision of a qualified mental health professional. Each chapter corresponds to a session or sessions of treatment and contains psychoeducational material in addition to homework assignments and self-assessments. Depending on the patient's and therapist's preferences, chapters in the patient workbook can be read before each session, better preparing the patient for what is to come. Alternatively, the patient can read relevant chapters after meeting with the therapist to reinforce points covered in the session. The patient can also refresh her memory concerning procedures covered in past sessions by reviewing workbook content. Moreover, patients can refer to the manual for guidance during the later phases of therapy, or after completing the treatment program. They can also use the workbook to share information with their friends and loved ones. Some patients appreciate the fact that their families can read portions of the manual and thus gain insight into the eating disorder and its treatment.

The workbook contains blank copies of all forms used throughout the program, including various self-monitoring records and worksheets for problem solving and cognitive restructuring. Patients will need multiple copies of some of the forms and are directed to the Treatments *That-Work*™ Web site (www.oup.com/us/ttw) where they can download extras. Alternatively, patients are encouraged to photocopy relevant forms directly from the workbook.

It is important to note that the workbook is not intended for use as a self-help manual without therapist guidance.

Chapter 2 | *Special Issues in Treatment*

Other Types of Purging

Laxatives

Many patients with bulimia nervosa use laxatives in addition to self-induced vomiting as a form of purging. More rarely, laxatives may be the only method of purging used. The most favored laxatives are those that stimulate the bowel, such as Correctol, and patients may use large amounts of these medications following a binge. It should be noted that laxatives are an extremely ineffective method of ridding the body of calories because most of the calories have been absorbed by the time the food reaches the lower bowel. At most, laxatives provide the illusion of "emptying the body" of excess calories. Experience suggests that the most effective method of dealing with the use of laxatives as a method of purging is to stop their use abruptly. The patient should be warned of the effects of stopping, which may include temporary constipation, bloating, and abdominal discomfort but can be reassured that such effects are relatively short-lived, being overcome in fewer than 10 days in most cases. A prescription for bulk laxatives or a diet high in fiber may help return the bowel to normal function. Some patients cannot tolerate the effects of suddenly stopping laxative use, usually because they fear the consequences in terms of weight gain. In such cases, laxatives should be withdrawn gradually on a schedule set in consultation with the patient. However, clinical experience suggests that gradual withdrawal is more problematic and less effective than abrupt withdrawal.

Diuretics

Less commonly, patients with bulimia nervosa abuse diuretics to decrease feelings of bloating and because they mistakenly believe they can better maintain their weight and shape this way. Chronic use of diuretics leads to renal damage and even renal failure, which requires dialysis. Patients who have used diuretics in large doses for a considerable period of time should be medically evaluated to ascertain their level of renal function. Experience suggests that abruptly stopping the diuretic is the best approach to this method of purging. Again, the patient should be warned that he or she might experience water retention, with bloating and the swelling of some body parts.

Ipecac

Occasionally, patients who have difficulty inducing vomiting use ipecac, a syrup that causes nausea and vomiting. Chronic use of ipecac is dangerous and may lead to cardiomyopathy (deterioration of the cardiac muscle) and heart failure. Because of these potential complications, patients should be advised to immediately stop using ipecac.

Exercise

Some patients with bulimia nervosa use exercise as their main method of controlling caloric intake (non-purging bulimia nervosa). Such exercise may be very vigorous, lasting for 2 hours or more, and may be pursued even if the patient is injured or feeling ill. In other words, such exercise is excessive, and the patient feels compelled to perform the exercise largely to allay shape and weight concerns. There is little evidence that the non-purging bulimic differs from the purging bulimic in any significant respect or that the results of treatment differ between the two groups. Because most bulimics also engage in dieting, the basic approach to treating the non-purging bulimic is the same as for the purging bulimic. Exercise may have to be gradually cut down as the eating pattern and concerns about shape and weight normalize. In addition, caloric intake may have to be increased to compensate for calories expended in excessive exercise.

Patients with bulimia nervosa should have a medical examination before beginning treatment. Although detailed medical investigations of patients with bulimia nervosa reveal only a few typical problems, some may be serious. The most frequent of these problems are dental and periodontal problems. Because of the sugars consumed and the acid that accumulates in the mouth upon vomiting, severe erosion of dental enamel may occur. In the more acute cases, metal fillings can be seen protruding from the tooth because the enamel around the filling has been eroded. Multiple dental caries (tooth decay that damages tooth structures) are often found in bulimic patients. Periodontal infections may also occur, sometimes with erosion of the bone surrounding teeth. If patients with bulimia nervosa are not seeing a dentist regularly, they should be advised to do so and to tell their dentist that they have bulimia nervosa. They should also be advised not to brush their teeth after purging because this may further damage enamel already softened by acid in the mouth. They are best advised to use a non-acidic, alkaline mouthwash after vomiting. The next most frequent problem is probably swelling of the salivary glands, giving a facial appearance that suggests the mumps. Such swelling is temporary and requires no treatment.

Dieting associated with bulimia nervosa not only reduces caloric intake but also the intake of needed minerals such as calcium, potassium, and magnesium, and vitamins, although outright vitamin deficiency is rarely seen in bulimia nervosa or binge-eating disorder. About 5% of patients with bulimia nervosa are found to have a low serum-potassium level (hypokalemia) due to purging. Hypokalemia may be associated with marked feelings of weakness, difficulty concentrating, and fainting. Low levels of potassium are associated with changes in the electrocardiogram. In combination with low weight, as may occur in the anorexic patient or the low-weight bulimic, a potassium deficiency may lead to fatal cardiac arrhythmia. Hypokalemia can be reversed with a prescription for a simple potassium supplement.

Fluid intake may also be reduced, leading to dehydration. In addition, because bulimics tend to avoid what they perceive as fattening foods, protein and fat intake may also be reduced. Some of these deficiencies are corrected by the amount and type of food eaten during binges;

hence, the picture is mixed, depending on the relative severities of dietary restriction and binge eating. Nonetheless, at the low-weight end of the spectrum, several important changes may occur. Blood pressure and heart rate may be lowered, giving rise to feelings of weakness, dizziness, and sometimes fainting. These events may be aggravated by the dehydration that accompanies food restriction, which is of course worsened by purging methods such as vomiting, using laxatives and diuretics, and exercising excessively. Calcium and protein deficiencies may lead to a reduction of bone density (osteopenia) and ultimately to osteoporosis. When osteopenia or osteoporosis is combined with excessive exercise, the risk of stress fractures is much increased. Occasionally, anemia may occur as a complication of dieting.

Because of the caloric and fluid restriction associated with dieting, thinking may become difficult and disorganized. In simple terms, there is not enough energy to fuel the normal functioning of the brain. This thinking difficulty may affect work performance and interpersonal relationships and may also interfere with psychotherapy. In addition, many bulimics find themselves continually thinking about dieting and binge eating. Such thoughts act as a distraction and may also interfere with work and other activities.

Rare complications include spitting up blood from small tears in the esophagus caused by purging. Cases of dilatation and, less commonly, stomach rupture have been reported following very large binges. Occasionally, this condition may lead to death. Foreign objects may also be swallowed in the course of a binge. For example, one of our patients swallowed a spoon in a particularly voracious eating episode, necessitating surgical removal.

Health Effects of Binge-Eating Disorder

Patients with binge-eating disorder tend to steadily gain weight, and many will become obese. It has been shown that as adiposity increases, the percentage of patients diagnosed with binge-eating disorder will increase. In most clinical samples, one quarter to one third of overweight individuals will meet criteria for binge-eating disorder. Hence, the medical complications associated with this disorder are those associated with overweight and obesity. It is now thought that binge-eating disorder and obesity are separate but overlapping disorders, probably with different risk factors, although they often run in families. Clearly, binge eating will lead to, or aggravate, overweight and obesity. Although stopping binge eating does not lead to weight loss in the short run, studies have shown that, over a longer term, those who stop binge eating are likely to weigh 10–15 lbs less than those who do not stop. Although this may not seem like a lot of weight to lose, the health effects of losing even 10 lbs can be significant. One problem for the binge eater is that dieting to lose weight will aggravate binge eating. Ultimately, dieting will lead to weight gain rather than weight loss. This is why it may be better to first overcome binge eating and then gradually develop healthy eating and exercise habits. This, of course, is very difficult to do in our modern world. In the United States, about 3,900 calories are produced by the food industry for every person in the country. This is almost double the caloric requirement for the average person. In addition, it is increasingly difficult to exercise enough. There are too few sidewalks in most communities, not all communities are safe to walk around, and almost no one can walk to work anymore. This is one of the reasons it is so difficult for overweight persons to lose weight and maintain losses.

Some of the medical problems associated with overweight and obesity are listed here, and many individuals with binge-eating disorder and overweight or obesity have more than one of these conditions. If the patient with binge-eating disorder does not have regular medical care, he or she should by referred for a medical examination. Medical risks include:

- High cholesterol levels (or high levels of triglycerides)

- High blood pressure

- Type 2 diabetes

- Heart disease (coronary artery disease)

- Stroke

- Gallbladder disease

- Osteoarthritis

- Sleep apnea

- Some cancers (endometrial, breast, and colon)

Issues Regarding Weight In Bulimia Nervosa

Patients with bulimia nervosa vary considerably in their weights, ranging from close to anorexic, with a body mass index (BMI) lower than 17.5, to the obese patient, with a BMI of 27 or higher. The latter group comprises some 10% of the clinical sample of bulimics. (In the U.S. customary system, BMI is calculated by dividing weight in pounds by height in inches squared and multiplying by 703. In the metric system, BMI is calculated as weight in kilograms, divided by height in meters squared.) Because weight and shape concerns are a cardinal feature of bulimia nervosa, patients at different points in this range will have different perceptions of the effects of treatment for their condition.

The Underweight Patient

Apart from the potential nutritional and health problems previously noted, the underweight patient often demonstrates marked resistance regarding the potential risk of weight gain once dietary restriction, purging, and excessive exercise are abandoned. Such patients may be excessively fearful of changing their eating habits in the first phase of treatment and may demonstrate less improvement than is usual during the first phase of therapy. Although the therapist can provide some reassurance regarding weight gain (that is, the average patient gains no weight following cognitive-behavioral therapy), the therapist must also point out that some weight gain for the underweight patient may occur as the patient begins to return to a biologically appropriate weight, and should have the patient examine the pros and cons of gaining a few pounds.

The Overweight Patient

Although the overweight patient with bulimia nervosa may not be as anxious about small weight gains as the markedly underweight patient, the overweight patient may also have unrealistic notions regarding weight loss, and hence run the risk of reinstating dieting with a subsequent relapse in binge eating and purging. Here, the argument can be made that the cycle of dieting, binge eating, and purging has not worked to maintain weight and has been accompanied by much misery in terms of preoccupation with food, anxiety, and guilt. The sensible alternative is to eat regularly, not to diet, and to adhere to a sensible exercise program. It has been our clinical experience that overweight patients will tend to lose some weight if they adhere to the cognitive-behavioral therapy prescriptions and that with cognitive restructuring they can more easily accept their body weight and shape.

The Patient with Binge-Eating Disorder

The patient with binge-eating disorder is in many ways similar to the overweight patient with bulimia nervosa. Because most of these patients come to the clinic seeking weight-loss treatment, they are often older than patients with bulimia nervosa. Therefore, it is important to screen clients presenting for the treatment of overweight and to suggest treatment for their binge-eating problem, which evidence suggests must be resolved before they have a chance to maintain their weight losses. There are two important differences in the treatment of these patients. First, clinical experience suggests that such patients will tend to gain weight during cognitive-behavioral treatment. To prevent this, it is suggested that some elements of a weight control program be added to the first phase of CBT. These should include weekly weighing (as for patients with bulimia nervosa) to track any weight gains; introducing a mild exercise program and adhering to that program; and gradually reducing fat in the diet. These elements appear to stop substantial weight gain during the course of CBT.

Patients who stop binge eating after completing CBT should then continue with a behavioral weight-loss program that incorporates elements of CBT. The aim is to achieve a sensible lifestyle without dietary restriction. Such a program may lead to average weight losses of 13–15 lbs. However, it should be emphasized, first, that these weight losses can be maintained and, second, that patients who do not abstain from bingeing will continue to gain weight—research has shown that the difference between the two groups at one-year post-treatment follow-up may be as much as 30 lbs. For those patients who do not stop binge eating, some alternative approaches are discussed in chapter 6 of the workbook.

Chapter 3 | *Pretreatment Assessment*

(Corresponds to chapter 1 of the workbook)

Before beginning treatment, it is necessary to evaluate the patient's complaints thoroughly. This can be done either by the professional who will become the patient's therapist, or by another professional, who will screen the patient. The format of Session 1 of cognitive-behavioral therapy will vary somewhat depending upon who assesses the patient because some of the initial fact gathering about the eating disorder will have been accomplished if the therapist assesses the patient. The assessment should cover three areas: the nature of the eating disorder, associated comorbid Axis I psychopathology, and comorbid Axis II psychopathology. In addition, the patient should be medically screened to investigate and/or treat common medical conditions such as hypokalemia (potassium deficiency) and anemia in the bulimic patient, and the medical problems associated with obesity in the patient with binge-eating disorder.

Assessing the Eating Disorder

This assessment can either be informal (e.g., a semi-structured screening interview) or formal, for example, using the Eating Disorder Examination developed by the group at Oxford and now considered the standard research and clinical instrument for the evaluation of eating-disordered patients. The best approach is to first ascertain the general nature of the eating disorder, that is, the presence or absence of binge eating and various types of purging, dietary restriction, and weight loss or gain. Questions to ask the patient include:

- Could you describe any episodes of overeating in the last month?

- What sorts of foods did you eat at that time?

- Did you feel out of control at that time (unable to stop eating)?

- Have you induced vomiting during the past month? What method(s) did you use to do that?

Similar specific questions should be asked about using laxatives and diuretics and about chewing and spitting. In each of these cases, you need to confirm that the reason the patient uses one or more of these methods is to purge calories or influence weight and/or shape. Also, determine the approximate length of time the patient has had the eating disorder; the dates of onset of dieting, binge eating, and purging; the patient's weight changes over the course of the illness; and any obvious precipitating factors. It is important to screen out patients meeting diagnostic criteria for anorexia nervosa (AN). Criteria for AN include a low body weight or a BMI of less than 17.5; a restricted eating pattern; a reported feeling of "fatness" in certain body parts (e.g., stomach, thighs, arms), despite being objectively underweight; a fear of gaining weight; and, in female patients, the absence of menstruation, bearing in mind that amenorrhea may be obscured in patients using contraceptive medication.

Once you have excluded the diagnosis of anorexia nervosa, take a careful history of the patient's binge-eating episodes. Help the patient classify the episodes as either "large" (objective) or "small" (subjective) and obtain an average number of objective binges over the last 4 weeks. Then, ascertain the average number over the past three months to determine if the patient meets the frequency criteria for bulimia nervosa. If the patient has been bingeing for more than three months, she may instead have binge-eating disorder. As noted earlier, in an objective binge, the bulimic consumes the caloric equivalent of about two meals (1,500 calories). Also examine the pattern of purging (if any) in detail, ascertaining the frequency (and dose, in the case of laxatives and diuretics) of each method used both at present and in the past. Whether or not the patient has used long periods of fasting to control weight or shape should also be ascertained. Examine the patient's exercise habits (directed at controlling weight and shape) in detail. Determine the type of exercise, the amount of exercise, and approximately how driven the exercise is. Discuss dietary restriction by having the patient recall the time of eating and the amount and type of food eaten in the last 24 hours and by inquiring about the typicality of the dietary pattern. The existence of food rules (rules about what and when to eat) should also be determined. Some bulimics defend their restricted-eating pattern by portraying it as vegetarian; however, the limited choices of foods and the dietary pattern (e.g., long intervals between eating, and the existence of food rules) reveal the restricted nature of the patient's food intake. Dietary patterns can be clarified by teaching the patient self-monitoring in the first session of CBT. The strength and nature of concerns about weight and shape should also be determined. Document patterns such as avoiding certain situations because of weight and shape concerns, repetitively pinching certain parts of the body to ascertain "fatness," and excessively looking in mirrors. Note both the behavior and the frequency of each behavior.

From the viewpoint of Axis I disorders, the most important conditions to evaluate are those commonly comorbid with eating disorders. These include depression, anxiety disorders, and substance dependence and abuse. The most commonly found Axis II disorders are aspects of the Cluster B personality disorders. The importance of ascertaining the presence of such a disorder is that the disorder may interfere with the therapy because of the patient's general impulsivity, disorganization, and tendency to form a hostile relationship with the therapist. As noted earlier, the two major contraindications to the treatment of bulimia nervosa and binge-eating disorder are the presence of a depression severe enough to stop the patient from fully engaging in therapy, and alcohol or drug dependence. Both of these conditions should be treated before beginning treatment of an eating disorder.

After establishing a diagnosis of either bulimia nervosa or binge-eating disorder, or a sub-threshold variant of either disorder severe enough to merit treatment, and having excluded anorexia nervosa, apprise the patient of the various options for treatment. Discuss the likelihood of success with each treatment, indicating that cognitive-behavioral therapy is the preferred treatment choice for bulimia nervosa and that CBT and IPT are equally effective for binge-eating disorder. Explain also that therapist-assisted self-help may be as effective as full CBT. This treatment may be especially helpful for the somewhat disorganized patient or the patient with less time to attend full sessions of CBT. You may briefly describe this time-limited therapy approach (see Chapter 16 for more information). In addition, you should ascertain the patient's motivation, pointing out that the treatment of an eating disorder takes considerable time and effort. Explain that those who do best in treatment are those who quickly make appropriate changes in their pattern of eating, that is, move to three meals and two snacks each day. Barriers to making such rapid changes should be examined. The patient's availability for treatment should also be examined. For example, flexibility in scheduling sessions, and any potential barriers to treatment should be explored. If the patient is interested in pursuing therapy, provide a copy of the corresponding workbook and instruct her to read chapter 1 and to complete the Bulimia and Binge-Eating Disorder Checklist and the Costs and Benefits Analysis worksheet to help assess her motivation for treatment.

The next section of the therapist guide details the first phase of cognitive-behavioral therapy. It is suggested that the therapist read both the therapist guide and the corresponding patient workbook before embarking on treatment.

Treatment Phase 1: Behavior Change

Chapter 4 | *Session 1*

(Corresponds to chapter 2 of the workbook)

Materials Needed

- Figure 1.1: A Model of Factors Maintaining Binge Eating and Purging
- Sample Daily Food Records

Session Outline

- If patient was evaluated before treatment and given the workbook, begin Session 1 by reviewing the homework
- Review the patient's history and personalize the CBT model of bulimia nervosa
- Provide the rationale for therapy and emphasize the importance of regularizing eating patterns
- Explain the three phases of treatment
- Outline the session structure
- Provide information on the likely outcome of treatment as indicated by the research literature
- Provide the rationale for self-monitoring and demonstrate how to use Daily Food Records
- Introduce the patient workbook
- Assign homework

Homework Review

As discussed in Chapter 1, it is important to conduct a pre-treatment evaluation of the patient before the first session. During the evaluation, the patient should have been instructed to read chapter 1 of the workbook. At the start of the session, check whether or not the patient has read the chapter and review her completed Checklist of Bulimia and Binge-Eating Disorder Symptoms and Costs and Benefits Analysis. In addition, address any questions the patient may have about the information presented in the workbook chapter.

Patient History and CBT Model

Briefly review the main findings of the patient's history, paying particular attention to the factors outlined in the cognitive-behavioral model of bulimia nervosa (see Figure 1.1). In particular, review the evidence supporting the link between concerns about weight and shape, dieting, binge eating, and purging needs, together with the effects of this behavior in (further) lowering feelings of self-esteem. Although there are individual differences, the patient with bulimia nervosa usually has a history compatible with the crucial elements of this schema, and it is useful for the therapist to draw the crucial elements of the model (as shown in Figure 1.1) on paper for the patient, illustrating how her history fits the model, and engage the patient in a discussion leading to at least an initial agreement that the model (or some parts of the model) fits her situation. Where possible, the patient's own words should be used in describing elements of the model. A particular focus should be on the effects of dieting, with some education about this topic. It may be useful to point out that when the body is starved of food, either by dieting alone or by combining dieting and excessive exercise, it will take over and demand food. This results in the patient's experiencing a loss of control over eating, which leads to a craving for high-calorie, high-fat foods. When this occurs, the patient usually ends up bingeing. Enough of the binge is kept down to maintain caloric balance, while the rest is purged. Because this is not an exact way to regulate caloric intake, weight may fluctuate, depending on how much food is absorbed or purged.

Given an initial, often reluctant, agreement that dieting driven by weight and shape concerns underlies the vicious cycle of binge eating and purging, the rationale for the first phase of treatment logically follows. Explain to the patient that the first aim of treatment will be to help normalize eating behavior. With your help, the patient will gradually work toward establishing a regular pattern of three meals and two snacks each day, eating by the clock, since the normal feelings of hunger and satiety no longer provide an accurate guide to food consumption in patients with eating disorders. Emphasize that all changes to be made throughout treatment will be made gradually. However, it is essential for the patient to take some risks, enduring the fear provoked by behaving differently (e.g., the fear of weight gain from eating regularly). Tell the patient that therapy is an excellent time to experiment with new behaviors and to observe the results of those behavior changes, and it provides her with an opportunity to obtain feedback and guidance from the therapist.

The patient may raise concerns at this point about potential weight gains using the prescribed regimen. Explain that the studies published to date show that, on average, patients gain at most a few pounds when they begin to regularize their eating patterns. This weight is usually due to the patient's overcoming dehydration (that is, it is "water weight"). In addition, reemphasize the way in which the body maintains caloric balance through binge eating and purging. Eating regularly is simply a way of reallocating the calories retained from binge eating.

Case Vignette

In the following example, T represents the therapist and P represents the patient.

T: It sounds like you were raised in a climate that really fosters some of your eating-disorder concerns. It sounds like your mom started you on diet pills and diuretics at a really young age, and she herself was contending with a weight problem and then overfeeding you, setting you up to be overweight and then to become, at a later date, hyper-focused on body weight and shape. I'm also hearing that your eating habits suggest a lot of restrictions. I mean, you're eating all the time, but you're also throwing up all the time, and I want you to look at this. I want you to look at this model (show Figure 1.1 CBT model of bulimia nervosa) and try to think about how your experience might resonate with it.

P. Low self-esteem concerning my shape and weight, that's probably pretty true.

T: How does the link between dieting and binge eating fit for you?

P: Binge eating and diet? I can't quite figure out how this goes with this. It certainly goes through sequentially.

T: What do you think of that aspect of the model? Can you relate to it?

P: Strict dieting, is it just caloric reduction, or is there more to it?

T: Great question. It's any kind of restriction. It can be the effect of vomiting all the time—you're leaving your body deprived or without energy or fuel. It can be reducing the overall amount of calories or limiting the number of eating episodes per day or having huge gaps between them. It can be limiting certain foods or food groups. All of the above contribute to a sense of feeling deprived. And you're doing all of the above.

P: You know what? I think I need to be on a diet. I see other people and think they don't need to be on a diet. I'm bigger than them.

T: Well, what happens when you deprive yourself in that way?

P: I don't lose weight.

T: Absolutely. So there are ways to both eat regularly and maintain your weight. One of them might be adopting a regimented amount of exercise, and another might be other things we can talk about later on, but basically the idea is first to interrupt the pattern of eating and purging. The pattern for you has been deprivation, deprivation, deprivation, and then a big binge because you throw up all day long. That's the first thing. Now it's a little bit naïve of me to say, now start eating regularly when you haven't been, but I think you need to take a stab at it by making a commitment to eat at least one sound meal over the next couple of days. Ideally, the pattern is breakfast, snack, lunch, snack, dinner, and maybe a snack separated by no more than two and half to three hours. That may be hard for you, but we really encourage you to take small steps toward that as the ideal.

Regularizing Eating Patterns

This advice forms the framework for the first phase of treatment. Given that the patient is experiencing abnormal sensations of hunger and fullness, suggest eating by the clock at regular intervals. You want the patient to work toward a pattern of consuming three meals and at least two snacks daily, with no gaps (during the waking day) between eating episodes longer than 3 hours. This usually means eating breakfast, a midmorning snack, lunch, an afternoon snack, and dinner. The afternoon snack is particularly important because the gap between lunch and dinner is often the longest interval between eating episodes during the day. Eating between these regular snacks and meals should be eliminated, and all eating episodes should be planned.

Restate the rationale for this plan. Tell the patient that stopping dieting will eventually lead to the cessation of binge eating and purging, and that a regular eating pattern will allow retraining of normal hunger and satiety sensations. Note that this change can be made gradually over the next few weeks. You may want to discuss with the patient a specific plan for the next day's food intake, examining scheduling problems that might interfere with this new eating pattern, and trying to solve such problems so that the beginnings of a specific plan will emerge.

The Three Phases of Treatment

The duration and structure of treatment was detailed in Chapter 1 and should be explained to the patient as outlined in that chapter. It is important for the patient to understand that there is a logical progression of treatment, beginning with establishing a regular pattern of eating, followed by expanding food choices and adding feared foods to the diet in appropriate quantities. As these aims are accomplished, the focus shifts to examining other triggers for binge eating, such as distorted thinking about food intake, weight, and shape that may be maintaining the eating disorder, and specific triggers for binge eating, for example, emotional triggers such as feeling upset after a faulty interpersonal interaction. You will eventually help the patient use problem-solving strategies to find solutions for overcoming these triggers.

In the final phase of treatment, you will examine the patient's residual problems, help identify ways of coping with them, and develop a plan for the months following treatment. If your patient suffers from binge-eating disorder, you will want to provide education about the link between binge eating and weight gain at this time as well. In addition, patients with binge-eating disorder should be informed that stopping binge eating is usually associated with a modest weight loss and that cognitive-behavioral therapy will include prescription of a mild exercise regimen and attention to the composition of the patient's diet.

You may use the following sample dialogue to facilitate discussion of the phases of treatment.

> *So, you might remember that the treatment is 20 sessions over 20 weeks. We're going to be meeting twice a week for the first 2 weeks, and then once a week until Session 16, and then every other week at the end. And, basically, the treatment is organized into three phases. The first 4, 6, or 8 weeks or so, we focus primarily on your behaviors and talk a lot about eating patterns and some related issues, things like activities you can do—instead of eating—when you're at risk for bingeing. We'll also address the issue of feared foods and how to include those in your diet. Then, midway through treatment, we'll talk more about some of the triggering components, what's setting you up to binge. Is it an attitude or a thought or concerns about shape or weight that lead you to binge? Are there problem situations or dilemmas that leave you baffled in terms of how to solve them, such that binge eating is the only solution? And then, toward the end of treatment, we'll address relapse prevention and helping you maintain gains you've made while you've been in treatment. And it's my expectation that you'll experience a lot of relief from your bingeing and purging by the time treatment is over. But there will probably still be more work to do. And most people can continue to improve on their own in the months following treatment, so that would be my expectation for you too.*

Session Structure

Using the information provided in Chapter 1, explain to the patient that well-structured sessions are integral to therapy. The usual structure dictates that, at the start of the session, the patient gives a brief overview of trends in eating behavior and purging, and any attempts made to change things. After this review, you and the patient will examine the issues in more detail using the patient's completed Daily Food Records to ascertain the details of each eating episode. You will then set an agenda for the remainder of the session, discuss new changes to try out, and make an agreement as to how to best achieve those changes. This will lead naturally to setting a specific homework task for the patient to complete before the next session, and usually to a review of what has been accomplished during the session. If necessary, you may alter the session structure. For example, if the patient experiences a crisis or emergency or has particular difficulty accepting an item of the agenda, you may need to address these issues up front at the start of the session. Nonetheless, in general, therapy progresses best when the agenda is set and accomplished and is consistent with the phase of therapy.

Treatment Outcome

Using the material in Chapter 1, provide the patient with some facts regarding the likely outcome of treatment. It is important that the patient know that cognitive-behavioral therapy has been tested in numerous controlled studies and has been found to be the most effective approach to the treatment of bulimia nervosa (and binge-eating disorder). Approximately 50% of patients who complete treatment will recover, and a further 25% will show very good improvement. Some of the latter group will also recover over the next few months if they continue to apply the principles learned during therapy. Hence, there is room for considerable optimism for improvement in the patient's eating disorder. You may also tell the patient that the results of treatment appear to be enduring. Follow-up studies of patients who have completed CBT suggest that most maintain their improvements. There may be occasional exacerbations of symptoms, in which case the patient should re-implement the strategies learned during treatment, or return for a few extra therapy sessions to quickly overcome the lapse.

Self-Monitoring

Explain to the patient the rationale for self-monitoring. Keeping detailed records of food intake, binge eating, purging, and exercise levels, in addition to other aspects of eating behavior, will help the patient become more aware of the exact pattern of the disturbed eating. Food records also provide information for the patient and therapist when they consider what changes need to be made. In addition, these records show the patient's progress over the course of treatment.

We provide two examples of a completed Daily Food Record in Figures 4.1 and 4.2—one for a patient with bulimia nervosa, and another for a patient with binge-eating disorder. The main difference between the two is that there is no purging column for the patient with binge-eating disorder but instead a column for recording planned exercise.

The patient should use this form daily, noting the day and date at the top. Column 1 is for noting the time any food or drink is taken. Column 2 is for recording which food(s) or liquid(s) were consumed. Each item should be noted as soon after consumption as possible. Calories should not be recorded. A simple description of the food and the amount eaten (in cups, ozs, etc.) is sufficient. Items comprising a meal should be enclosed in parentheses. Column 3 is for recording the place where the food was consumed. Column 4 is for noting eating episodes that the patient considered to constitute a binge. In the version for bulimic patients, Column 5 is for recording purging behaviors, whether they be self-induced vomiting, laxative use (note type and amount), or diuretics (note type and amount). For binge-eating patients, Column 5 is for recording exercise. Column 6 is the comments column and is used to note events that influenced eating (e.g., hunger, an argument that led to binge eating.)

Depending on your patient's diagnosis, show her either Figure 4.1 (a sample record for the bulimic patient) or Figure 4.2 (a sample record for the binge-eating patient) and emphasize the need for accuracy in re-

Time	Food and Liquid Consumed*	Location	Binge?	Purge?	Comments
8:00 am	1 cup Coffee, half a banana	Kitchen			I was rushed
11:15 am	Nestle chocolate bar	Desk			Bought it a few days ago and left in my desk, bad but easy.
2:15 pm	Kraft Mac and Cheese Diet coke—half a can	Desk			Couldn't get out for lunch, not excessive eating but not good for me either
6:00 pm	2 wafer cookies with chocolate filling	Desk			
7:30 pm	4 KFC spicy breaded chicken strips, 1/4 cup of BBQ beans, 2 cups of corn with butter, 2 biscuits, ranch dressing, 1 pint of ice cream	In front of TV	Binge	Vomited	Had a quarrel with my boyfriend on the phone before this. Felt angry and resentful.

Figure 4.1

Example of Completed Daily Food Record for Bulimic Patient

porting (e.g., amounts of food or liquid consumed, time of day consumed). You may explain these further in subsequent sessions when examining the patient's own records.

Patient Workbook

Discuss with the patient how to use the corresponding workbook. The workbook reinforces educational material covered in the sessions, and also clarifies therapeutic procedures. The patient can review the chapters after particular sessions, can review pertinent chapters if she is having difficulty with a particular area, and can refer to the manual after treatment has been completed. In addition, some patients find the workbook useful for educating family members about the disorder and about treatment. Each chapter corresponds to a particular session (or sessions) of treatment and contains homework exercises and self-assessments.

Time	Food and Liquid Consumed	Location	Binge?	Exercise	Comments
7:45 am	2 slices of bread with jam	kitchen		10 minute walk	A little hungry, just wanted to eat enough to last to lunch time
10:30 am	1 can diet Pepsi				
11:30 am	8 thin mints, 2 cups of cheese nips, 3 pieces of pizza 2 glasses of water	office	Binge		Started with the cookies, it's hopeless! I really don't like working here. I am out of control. I'll never lose weight
1:30 pm	15 Hershey's Kisses	office	Binge		Falling asleep, need sugar or something, don't want this, I'm not hungry
6:30 pm	2 thick peanut butter sandwiches, 2 glasses of milk				I want to stuff myself, out of control. I'm getting tired of this. I am alone.

Figure 4.2

Example of Completed Daily Food Record for Binge-Eating Patient

Finally, ask if the patient has any questions about the treatment. Answer the questions completely and comprehensively. If the queries are related to a concept to be introduced in a later session, provide a brief answer now and return to it during the relevant session.

Homework

✎ Instruct the patient to begin self-monitoring using the Daily Food Record in chapter 3 of the workbook. (Note: The patient will not be asked to read chapter 3 in its entirety until the next session. For now, simply refer the patient to the Daily Food Record on pages 49–50.)

✎ Have the patient read chapter 1 of the workbook and complete the chapter exercises and self-assessment if these were not done before this session.

✎ Ask the patient to read chapter 2 of the workbook and complete the self-assessment.

(Corresponds to chapter 3 of the workbook)

Materials Needed

- Weight Change Record (for binge-eating patients only)

Session Outline

- Review the patient's homework

- Review the link between dieting and binge eating and the rationale for establishing regular eating patterns

- Reinforce the patient's attempts to regularize her eating and examine ways to help her expand on new behaviors

- Introduce weekly weighing and educate the patient about body weight

- Assign homework

  It is useful for the therapist to set an agenda for each session, either writing it into the progress notes or recording it on tape. An example follows:

  > This is February 27th, session number 2 with patient 2110. My plan for the session today is to review her Daily Food Records in depth, looking for her patterning in eating, supporting the CBT model where appropriate, and being sure that the instructions for monitoring were clear. Then I will introduce weekly weighing, handle issues about weight, if necessary, and make that a homework assignment.

  Writing down or otherwise noting the agenda for the session allows the therapist to check back at the end of the session to see if the agenda was accomplished and to ascertain the reasons for any drift away from the agenda.

Homework Review

Because the patient's Daily Food Records are a central aspect of therapy, it is important to pay detailed attention to them during the initial part of Session 2. After greeting the patient and asking a general question as to how things have gone since the last session, review her completed food records meal by meal. There are several reasons for this. The first is to reinforce the record keeping. Paying attention to the patient's completed records and recognizing their importance will help accomplish this. Positive feedback regarding well-kept records is also helpful. The second reason for reviewing records is to look for omissions and identify any difficulties the patient may have had in keeping her records (e.g., neglecting to record food quantities accurately) and to help the patient correct such problems. Take note of major problems, such as incomplete record keeping, and follow up with the patient after the initial review. The third purpose of the record review is to obtain a more accurate view of the patient's eating behavior, including meals, snacks, binges, and purges. In particular, pay close attention to the timing of eating episodes. If the amounts of food consumed or the time of eating are unclear from the records, have the patient clarify these, and use this opportunity to remind the patient of the importance of accurate record keeping. The final purpose of this initial review is to use the information to reinforce the relevance of the cognitive-behavioral model for the patient. You can do this by looking for long periods of food deprivation followed by binge eating, and pointing out the relationship between such deprivation and binge eating. This can also help "normalize" binge eating by pointing out that the patient is simply compensating—eating a large amount of food in the form of a binge—for the previous caloric deficit caused by dieting. Defining the relationship between dietary restriction and binge eating allows the therapist to repeat the rationale for the work of the first phase of treatment, namely, to move the patient step-by-step toward eating three meals and two snacks each day at regular intervals.

Time	Food and Liquid Consumed*	Location	Binge?	Purge?	Comments
9:30	1 bowl of soup	kitchen			
2:00	tuna sandwich				
6:30	chocolate chip cookies with coffee				

Figure 5.1

Example of Completed Session 2 Daily Food Record for Bulimic Patient

The sample completed Daily Food Record shown in Figure 5.1 depicts the first day of self-monitoring in a patient with bulimia nervosa who demonstrates a very restricted pattern of eating and long gaps between eating episodes. This patient reports just three eating episodes in the day, with gaps of 4.5 hours between each episode. In addition, only the lunchtime episode approximates a normal meal. In fact, the record is so sparse that the therapist might wonder if items have not been recorded, but at this early point in therapy it would probably be a mistake to question the patient regarding missing items. This record can be used to emphasize the role of dietary restriction in maintaining binge eating and purging—referring to the cognitive-behavioral model of bulimia, and to note the long delays between meals. In fact, the day after this long interval of restriction, the patient binged and purged several times. This particular patient might also be encouraged to make some notes in the comments column. Finally, you might gently nudge the patient to record the number of cookies eaten at 6:30 P.M.

Weekly Weighing

Patients with bulimia nervosa and binge-eating disorder either weigh themselves too frequently, thus becoming demoralized over small weight gains that have no meaning, or entirely avoid weighing themselves. Introduce the notion of weekly weighing in the context of education about weight changes that might be expected during the course of treatment. Most studies of cognitive-behavioral therapy for bulimia nervosa have found that, on average, patients either experience no weight gain or gain only 2 or 3 lbs. You can use this information to assuage the patient's fears that, when she begins to eat more normally, she will lose control of her weight. It is important to note, however, that the average may be misleading; some patients lose weight and others gain weight. Regardless, the point is that treatment will help move the patient toward a more natural weight.

Point out to the patient that her present behavior has many costs, including constant preoccupation with food, guilt about binge eating and purging, and the effect that such behavior has on her relationships with people (whether she hides her behavior or not) and on her health (e.g., the effects of vomiting on teeth). The amount of time the disorder consumes often isolates the patient from others, leading to deteriorating interpersonal relationships. It seems reasonable to trade these disadvantages for the risk that she might gain some weight as she achieves a more natural weight.

The overweight patient may be particularly concerned about possible weight gain because such an individual may have been fighting a losing battle against weight for a long time. The argument to make in such cases is that the patient's bulimic behavior has not been successful in helping reduce weight and has resulted in many negative effects. Hence, it seems reasonable to take the risk of changing the behavior and seeing what happens to her weight. You might mention that as treatment progresses the problem of the patient's weight will not be forgotten and that a sensible weight-control program will gradually be developed if needed. Moreover, it has been our clinical experience that overweight patients with bulimia nervosa tend to lose some weight when they stop binge eating and purging.

The underweight patient may also be markedly concerned about weight gain. Many of these individuals are recovered anorexics or borderline anorexics and have very strong concerns about weight and shape. These patients present a difficult therapeutic problem, particularly because low weight seems to be a factor predicting a poor outcome from treatment. The cost–benefit analysis discussed in Chapter 3 highlights eating-disorder symptoms versus risks of weight gain and may be useful when dealing with such patients. The underweight patient should view the treatment as an experiment and commit to take the risk of learning to live differently.

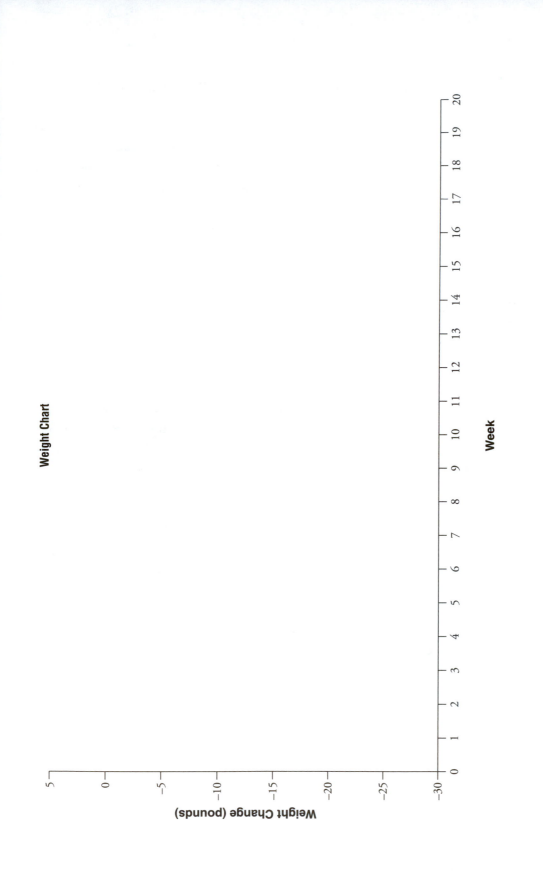

Weight Chart

Weight Change (pounds)

Week

For patients with binge-eating disorder (but not those with bulimia nervosa), it is suggested that they plot their weight each week on the Weight Chart on page 55. This will provide the longer term feedback that will help them control their weight. This chart is not included in the patient workbook because the patient with bulimia nervosa should not plot her weight: the objective for bulimics is to *lessen* their concern about weight. For purposes of distribution, you may photocopy this form from the book or download multiple copies from the Treatments *That Work*™ Web site at www.oup.com/us/ttw.

Self-Disclosure

A few years ago, it was usual for patients with bulimia nervosa to hide their binge eating and purging from everyone, even those with whom they lived. This situation has changed because the media has educated the public and there is now better acceptance of eating disorders. However, some patients continue to hide their behavior from everyone. It is useful to inquire about whether or not the patient has confided in anyone (e.g., a spouse or best friend) about her eating disorder. If the patient has not, explore the reasons and discuss the advantages of disclosure. Making the disorder known to those close to the patient can provide extra motivation for the patient to improve because the disorder is made more real through disclosure. In addition, the patient can be relieved of some of the burden of guilt and the need to deceive those with whom the patient lives.

The Patient with Binge-Eating Disorder

Binge-eating patients generally range from overweight to seriously obese. It is clear that stopping binge eating and implementing a sensible weight-control program allows these patients to lose a little weight, but, more importantly, it permits them to stabilize their weight.

A Daily Food Record for a patient with binge-eating disorder is shown in Figure 5.2. This record is fairly typical for such patients, who tend to eat larger meals than bulimics. However, as can also be seen, this patient

Time	Food and Liquid Consumed	Location	Binge?	Exercise	Comments
8:10 a.m.	Kool-Aid – 32 oz	at desk			Weighed 225lbs; didn't sleep well, so feeling tired and kind of moody; depressed. A little hungry—felt like I should eat breakfast.
8:30 a.m.	coffee w/2 Teaspoons of non-fat milk & a little bit of hot chocolate mix Non-fat Yogurt – 8 oz. 1 cup Rice Chex cereal				
10:30 a.m.	1 apple, more coffee	at desk			hungry, wanted something to eat
11:10 a.m.	2 rice cakes (Roman Meal)	at desk			kind of hungry
1:00 p.m.	a little less than 1 pint chicken and rice soup from Chinese food restaurant 1 rice cake 1/2 artichoke 2 diet cokes (24 oz. total)	at desk			Lunchtime, hungry Didn't like seeing oil in soup. Tried to eat around it. That's why I didn't eat it all. Still feel a little hungry and still feeling down.
1:40 p.m.	2 Hershey's kisses	at desk			Craving chocolate
1:50 p.m.	1 oz peanut M&M's (about 14)	at desk			I'm feeling like I may binge later today. I'm tired.
3:00 p.m.	1 med apple	at desk			think I might be hungry Still want to eat
8:50 p.m.	2 slices lemon meringue pie, 1 bite cake	Mom's kitchen	Binge		
10:00 p.m.	1 large piece pie 1 piece cake Double scoop of Baskin Robbins Ice Cream	in car in car and in room	Binge		Thought a little about having to weigh myself in am and a little nervous

Figure 5.2

Example of Completed Session 2 Daily Food Record for Binge-Eating Patient has no real dinner; hence, exactly the same points about regular eating that were suggested for the patient with bulimia nervosa can be made for the patient with binge-eating disorder. From the comments column, we can see that this patient is probably weighing herself every morning.

Homework

✎ The patient should continue working toward a regular pattern of eating three meals and two snacks per day.

✎ The patient should continue self-monitoring using the Daily Food Record.

✎ Instruct the patient to begin weighing herself weekly at the same time of day each week and recording her weight in the comments column of the Daily Food Record.

✎ Have the patient read chapter 3 of the workbook and complete the self-assessment.

Chapter 6 *Session 3*

(Corresponds to chapter 4 of the workbook)

Session Outline

▪ Review the patient's homework

▪ Continue to encourage regular eating patterns in the patient

▪ Educate the patient about dietary restriction, hunger, and satiety to help reinforce regular eating

▪ Discuss self-induced vomiting and why it is ineffective as a calorie-reduction technique

▪ If applicable, educate the patient about laxative abuse

▪ Encourage the patient to engage in pleasant activities incompatible with binge eating

▪ Prescribe an exercise regimen for the patient with binge-eating disorder

▪ Assign homework

Homework Review

Review the patient's completed Daily Food Records, noting the days on which records were well kept and also helping correct any deficiencies in the records, such as missing descriptions of quantities of food, food types, times of eating episodes, and so on. The therapist should note areas pertinent to the main topic of the session for further review after the agenda is set. At this point, you should begin to involve the patient in the review of her records, for example, asking the patient to talk about

Time	Food and Liquid Consumed*	Location	Binge?	Purge?	Comments
8:50 a.m.	Latte	car			hungry, rushed, running late
12:30 p.m.	Veggie hotdogs, chips	living room TV			hungry
2:00 p.m.	1 piece of chocolate	shopping			
4:30 p.m.	2 pieces of chocolate	shopping			I usually eat 3, so I was still craving a third. Felt a little guilty
6:30 p.m.	Popcorn Coffee – pot of decaf	TV living room			not really hungry craving popcorn
11:30 p.m.	Bowl of cereal	kitchen			hungry, sort of

Figure 6.1

Example of completed Session 3 Daily Food Record for Bulimic Patient

what she has noted since the last session. Eventually, much of the record review should be generated by the patient rather than by the therapist.

An example of a Daily Food Record for a patient with bulimia nervosa is shown in Figure 6.1. This record demonstrates both dietary restriction and long gaps between meals. For example, between 12:30 P.M. and 6:30 P.M., the patient ate only three pieces of chocolate. There are no episodes of binge eating, and the amount of food eaten is clearly insufficient, leading the patient to experience hunger for much of the day. A record like this would afford an excellent opportunity to discuss the effects of delaying eating and could lead to problem solving with the patient. When reviewing the record, the therapist might also ask about the amount of popcorn eaten at 6:30 P.M. and the size of the bowl of cereal, underlining the importance of accurately monitoring portion sizes.

Dealing with Unusual Schedules

Night workers often have difficulty regularizing their eating. Women with a family are especially affected because they often have to prepare meals for the family, and also eat regularly while at work. The following example illustrates the difficulties with a patient who is a night nurse.

In the following example, T represents the therapist and P represents the patient.

T: How do you think your work affects your eating?

P: It's just that I'm on the job for 8 hours. You don't have your standard two 10–15 minutes and an hour and a half break so that you can regroup. You have to eat while you're still attending to a patient. If they call you, you don't have a lunch per se. You eat, but you don't have a lunch to get your mind to focus. That part of the job makes eating a little complicated. Trying to get it in order.

T: Do you feel you just don't have control over your eating process because you don't get to decide when you eat?

P: I think so. I think that it plays a part. You gotta eat when you can. Or a patient wakes up and they're on morphine or there is a morphine drip. And they need to be changed, cleaned, depending on their physical being, I've had 12-hour shifts and haven't eaten for 6 hours, and you finally sit down and eat, and in the middle of eating, the demand is still on you.

T: So, you feel like it's really hard to relax when you eat?

P: You gotta eat fast so you can have a decent meal, and then you're sitting here kind of stuck, kind of full, but then you don't know what to expect. At least in this particular job. I don't know if this kind of eating behavior also depends on occupation.

In this example, there are several problems to solve over the next few weeks. First, the therapist must help the patient better organize the night routine. Part of this may involve encouraging the patient to be more assertive about having regular breaks. Suggest that she ask for another nurse to relieve her while she has her meal. In addition, help her plan ahead and prepare snacks to bring to work to eat at specific times. In this situation, it may take several weeks of problem solving before regular eating patterns are established.

The next part of the session focuses on education regarding dieting, self-induced vomiting, and laxative use (if applicable). It is often helpful to explore the patient's beliefs regarding these issues (particularly self-induced vomiting and laxative use) before providing corrective information.

Dietary Restriction, Hunger, and Satiety

The purpose of educating the patient about dietary restriction, hunger, and satiety is to reinforce the concept of regularizing eating patterns and overcoming other forms of dieting. Long-term dieting leads to several problems. First, the pattern of food intake tends to become irregular, often with long gaps between meals; or sometimes the pattern is chaotic, with numerous small eating episodes during the day. Second, dieting is associated with a restriction in the variety of food eaten and is accompanied by rules about what to eat and what not to eat. When control breaks down, the patient tends to eat foods that are forbidden by the dietary rules, and the enjoyment of eating these foods combined with the guilt over breaking food rules sets up a vicious cycle of further dieting and binge eating. Third, the experience of hunger, which should normally precede a meal, tends to be experienced either almost all day because of the caloric deficit secondary to dieting, or else not experienced when it might be expected to, that is, after not eating for several hours. Fourth, because the size of meals varies when one is dieting and binge eating, and because the patient purges, the experience of satiety or fullness is disrupted. Patients often feel full after eating only a small amount of food, or may feel full only after very large eating episodes. Patients can no longer rely on their internal feelings of hunger and satiety to regulate eating. This is why regularizing eating patterns and eating by the clock is so important.

In essence, strict dieting leads to a caloric deficit, which the patient's physiology tries to compensate for through a large eating episode. Such episodes (which can be viewed as normal compensation) are experienced as a binge, with all the concomitant feelings of feeling out of control, anxious or depressed, and then guilty. Purging, while it does rid the body of calories, is not particularly effective, as noted in Chapter 2, because calories can be absorbed quite quickly from the stomach.

Self-Induced Vomiting

Self-induced vomiting provides few benefits and is associated with a number of health hazards. Nutrients, including calories, from food that is eaten are quickly absorbed through the stomach. Although many bulimics believe they are able to purge most of the calories they have eaten, this is simply not true. A sizable fraction of calories consumed in a binge are, in fact, absorbed. Self-induced vomiting is an inefficient method of ridding the body of calories. Moreover, eating followed by purging and often followed by another binge and more purging leads the body to give false signals regarding hunger and satiety. Patients who purge receive faulty feedback from their bodies about their nutritional status. Internal regulatory mechanisms then take control, "forcing" the bulimic to make up for the chronic caloric deprivation. Such eating episodes are experienced as being out of the patient's control and are labeled as a binge.

This form of purging also has undesirable health consequences. Of these, the most important may be dental decay caused by acid in the mouth from vomiting combining with the sugars from typical binge foods. In a small proportion of patients, potassium is depleted from the body, with undesirable consequences on cardiovascular function. In some patients, there is marked swelling of the salivary glands, giving an appearance of "mumps." Discuss with the patient all these reasons for stopping purging.

Laxative Abuse

Patients who are abusing laxatives as a form of purging should first be educated about the problems with laxative abuse. Laxative abuse is not an effective method of ridding the body of calories. In fact, it is the least effective method. All the caloric content of food has been absorbed by the time food is in the part of the intestinal tract that is emptied by laxatives. Laxative use leads to cycles of dehydration and rehydration and so aggravates negative feelings about body shape. In addition, stimulant laxatives reduce the normal contractions of the intestines, making it necessary for patients to continue using them to avoid constipation.

The best method to treat laxative abuse is to have the patient stop the laxatives abruptly and throw away all her supplies. Slowly cutting back on laxative use simply prolongs the side effects of laxative withdrawal. Explain to the patient that she will probably experience discomfort for 10–14 days, including constipation, bowel discomfort and cramping, and a temporary weight gain due to rehydration. Explain also that most patients who use laxatives have relatively little trouble stopping. Suggest simple methods of treating constipation, such as consuming additional bran, fruit, and salads. For patients who refuse to quit abruptly or who have trouble following this regimen, suggest a scheduled reduction of laxatives over a 10-day period, together with the substitution of a bulk laxative, if needed. Such a schedule should be developed and individualized with the patient's help.

Alternative Activities to Binge Eating and Purging

During treatment it is often helpful to have the patient devise activities that are incompatible with binge eating and to use them to handle urges to induce vomiting, particularly when binges are of the subjective type. Although objective binge episodes may disappear, leaving only subjective binges, such binges are often accompanied by uncomfortable feelings, such as being over-full, and may therefore lead to purging.

Encourage the patient to consider activities that are incompatible with binge eating and purging and to compile a list of such activities that she can incorporate into her life. For example, when faced with an urge to binge, the patient might leave the environment in which the urge has occurred and go for a walk, call a friend, or engage in some other type of distracting activity. It should be noted that patients often choose alternative activities that are not particularly pleasant. Such alternatives are not especially useful in the long run. It is important to help the patient identify activities that are both incompatible with binge eating and purging and that are also pleasurable. For example, as part of a formal problem-solving exercise, you might get the patient to develop a list of activities and then rank them based on how pleasurable they are. You may have to teach the patient the following problem-solving steps:

Step 1: *Identify the problem as specifically as possible.* Here the aim is to be able to write down a specific problem.

Step 2: *List alternative solutions to the problem.* Encourage the patient to brainstorm and list as many different solutions to the problem as possible without regard to their practicality. The important aspects of this step are to make sure that the patient really thinks out the various alternatives and to ensure that the patient does not prematurely rule out potentially viable solutions. This may be difficult for many patients because they have rigid ways of dealing with problem situations. At times you may need to suggest an alternative behavior if it seems fairly obvious, simply to enlarge the list of choices. It should be noted that binge eating and purging may appear in the patient's list of solutions. It is important to allow the patient to consider the practicality and effectiveness of binge eating and purging together with the other solutions listed. Considering these may lead to a productive analysis of the costs and benefits of binge eating and purging.

Step 3: *Evaluate the solutions.*

Step 4: *Choose one or more solutions to the problem based on the evaluation.*

Step 5: *Follow through on the solution.* Here it is necessary for the patient to note each time she uses this particular method to solve a problem and for the therapist to follow up by asking the patient about the problem and solution in future sessions.

Step 6: *Reevaluate the problem and solutions.* After implementing the solution, the patient should consider the degree of success associated with the solution and, if necessary, revisit the problem-solving procedure to fine-tune the process or to find other solutions.

Note: Chapter 11 of the workbook is dedicated to the problem-solving method. You may wish to refer the patient to this chapter now or you may assign it for reading homework at the start of Phase 2 of treatment.

The advice regarding regular eating and engaging in activities incompatible with bingeing is as central to the patient with binge-eating disorder as it is to the patient with bulimia nervosa. In addition, it is important to give the patient advice regarding establishing a regular exercise program. Patients with binge-eating disorder tend to put on weight during cognitive-behavioral therapy; hence, it is important to combine some of the elements of a weight-control program with cognitive-behavioral therapy. These include having patients weigh themselves weekly (as is done with bulimic patients), plot their weight change on the Weight Chart (see Chapter 5), institute a regular exercise program, and cut down on the amount of fat consumed.

Unlike the patient with bulimia nervosa, most patients with binge-eating disorder do not exercise regularly, if at all. The first step is to examine the frequency and duration of the exercise that the binge-eating patient records in the exercise column of the Daily Food Record. The most promising and least costly exercise program is brisk walking for at least 30 minutes a day no fewer than 4 days a week. For the patient who has never exercised, develop a graduated schedule. For example, 10 minutes of moderate-paced walking four times a week, or 30 minutes of moderate-paced walking one or two times a week. Instruct the patient to wear comfortable shoes and begin the walking program at a time that will fit into her schedule and be likely to be maintained. If the patient has the equipment, then a stationary bicycle, treadmill, elliptical machine, or such can be used instead. The aim is to develop a convenient and pleasurable exercise program that will be maintained. Occasionally, you will have a patient who has already been exercising more than the amount suggested here. Use your judgment to determine whether to increase the amount of exercise or to encourage the patient to continue at the same level.

Homework

✎ The patient should continue working toward a regular eating pattern of three meals and two snacks per day.

✎ Instruct the patient to continue self-monitoring using the Daily Food Record.

✎ Instruct the patient to continue to weigh herself weekly and record her weight on the Daily Food Record.

✎ The patient should begin to engage in pleasurable alternative activities.

✎ If problem solving was discussed during the creation of the activity list, you may wish to refer the patient to chapter 11 of the workbook.

✎ Direct the binge-eating patient to incorporate the agreed-upon exercise routine into her daily schedule.

✎ Have patient read chapter 4 of the workbook and complete chapter exercises and self-assessment

Chapter 7   *Session 4*

(Corresponds to chapter 5 of the workbook)

Session Outline

- Review the patient's homework

- Clarify and review the CBT model of bulimia, the concept of weekly weighing, and any other material not fully covered in Session 3, if necessary

- Address any emerging problems with treatment compliance

- Assign homework

Homework Review

The outline for Session 4 and all subsequent sessions will follow the same sequence. The principal focus of these sessions is the patient's completed Daily Food Records. Remember, allow the patient to gradually take the lead in reviewing her records while you take note of items to be discussed. Focus mainly on the patient's pattern of eating. Up to this point, the sample Daily Food Records provided in this guide have shown fairly typical patients with relatively long intervals between eating episodes. The aim for these types of patients is to shorten these intervals with the prescription of three meals and two snacks each day.

Another typical eating pattern is illustrated in the sample Daily Food Record shown in Figure 7.1. This patient ate frequently between 10:40 A.M. and 2:55 P.M., then there was a 6-hour interval during which she ate only one carrot before binge eating at 8:50 P.M. This illustrates two problems. First, the record is a nice example of a long interval between eating episodes leading to binge eating, emphasizing the importance of eating "by the clock." Second, this record, from 10:40 A.M. to 3:00 P.M., illustrates a pattern of grazing. In this case, the patient needs to begin to group the eating episodes into three meals and two snacks daily.

Time	Food and Liquid Consumed	Location	Binge?	Purge?	Comments
10:40 a.m.	1 apple	living room			woke up @ 10:30 hungry
11:00 a.m.	1 cup Bran flakes 1/4 cup grape nuts 1/3 cup Mueslix 1/2 banana 1 cup non-fat milk	living room			Breakfast
12:30 p.m.	Diet Coke				
1:30 p.m.	French bread pizza w/ light mozzarella cheese, mushrooms, olives, onion & zucchini (about 2") Diet Coke	backyard			Think I'm hungry— want to eat because I plan to go on a bike ride later
2:55 p.m.	1/3–1/2 power bar water	living room			a little hungry, don't want to get hungry on ride Rode bike 1 1/2 hrs.
5:40 p.m.	1 carrot	walking around			hungry, tasted good
8:50 p.m.	Rice with leftover Szechwan shrimp (about 3 cups) Diet Coke 1 iced coffee 1 small non-fat, sugar-free yogurt	living room			hungry
	Special K (1 bowl) 3 bowls of bran flakes with milk 1 cup Mueslix 3/4 cup non-fat milk	kitchen living room	Binge	Vomited	tired, but want to eat something not hungry, but still wanted it.

Figure 7.1

Example of Completed Session 4 Daily Food Record for Bulimic Patient

Problems with adhering to the treatment program are likely to emerge in the first phase of treatment and should be promptly handled as obstacles to progress. Among the problems are poor attendance, incomplete food records, failure to do homework, failure to take risks to change, and challenging the model or advice. In general, the problem needs to be directly addressed with the patient, the reasons for the problem explored, and solutions generated.

Poor Attendance

This may consist of missing sessions with little or no warning, or coming late to sessions. Many patients with bulimia nervosa lead a somewhat disorganized life, resulting in attendance problems. It may be necessary to explore the reasons for absence or tardiness in some detail and to help the patient arrive at a solution to the problem. It is possible that such patients, who often have fewer life resources, would do better with the therapist-assisted self-help treatment program (See Chapter 16) because it makes fewer demands on their time.

Another possibility is that patients with marked avoidant traits may feel uncomfortable in therapy. Particularly if they feel they are not meeting their perfectionist standards, they may expect criticism from the therapist for these perceived failings. Such patients frequently arrive late or miss sessions altogether to avoid the painful feelings evoked in therapy. It may be necessary to problem solve with this type of patient, correcting her erroneous beliefs about the therapy situation and the therapist's view of her.

Finally, it may be that the patient is not ready to commit enough effort for therapy to be successful. This issue can be usefully explored by examining the Costs and Benefits Analysis the patient completed before the first session (see Chapter 3). This may help the patient resolve the problem, either by helping her recognize that she is not yet ready for therapy or by encouraging a commitment of more time and effort to treatment.

Resistance to Record Keeping

Although most patients will need some help keeping their records satisfactorily, they are usually able to accomplish the task with relative ease. A few patients may pose a greater problem by resisting record keeping altogether, possibly stating that they are unable to keep such records. These patients are often afraid that the therapist will criticize them for their "bad eating behavior," about which they feel deeply ashamed. These patients are often socially phobic individuals, intimidated by authority figures, whom they view as critical, unpredictable persons. A gentle but thorough exploration of these attitudes, thoughts, and feelings is important to help the patient begin to resolve the problem. It may be helpful to point out to the patient that her disorder is common and that she is no different from other patients with the same problem. Also, it may be necessary to shape the patient's record keeping step-by-step. For example, you may encourage her to keep a complete and detailed Daily Food Record for just one day. As she gains confidence, instruct her to begin keeping records for multiple days. Other patients are able to keep the records but are not willing to show them to the therapist. If this occurs, have the patient share her information by reading it to you. As she becomes more comfortable, she will eventually be able to show you her written records.

As was the case with the patient who arrives late or misses sessions, it may be that failure to keep records is associated with a lack of resources or an insufficient commitment to therapy.

Failure to Comply with Behavior-Change Advice

It is essential that patients complete the homework agreed upon at the end of each session. Behavior change has to occur in the patient's own environment, making it necessary for her to try out new behaviors and observe and document the results of such behavior change through self-monitoring. Failure to comply with behavior-change advice may stem from several causes. First, the changes agreed upon may be too difficult for the patient to undertake. If this is the case, then the therapist and patient need to break down the behavior changes into smaller steps and set smaller goals for homework. Second, the patient may not have fully absorbed the personal implications of the cognitive-behavioral model of bulimia nervosa or some aspect of the educational efforts outlined in previous chapters. This can be remedied by outlining the model in different ways using data from the patient's self-monitoring records and history to illustrate how the model specifically applies to her. Third, the patient may not be able to take the risk to change her behavior, fearing that the consequences (e.g., weight gain) may be catastrophic. In this case, address the patient's feared consequences realistically, at the same time pointing out that the patient's present behavior is painful and damaging to her in many ways. Here again, an analysis of the patient's personal costs and benefits may be useful. It may also be useful to explore the patient's thoughts connected with her failure to follow the program. Additionally, it may be useful to introduce cognitive restructuring, even at this early point in therapy. Education and persuasion extending over several sessions may be needed to overcome the problem of reluctance to risk behavior changes. Therapy cannot work without the patient's taking risks to make appropriate behavior changes.

The Patient Who Challenges the Model or Prescriptions

One of the most difficult problems confronting a therapist is the patient who continually challenges either the basic cognitive-behavioral model of bulimia nervosa or each and every prescription made by the therapist, questioning their usefulness and applicability to the patient. Such patients often have a comorbid personality disorder that contributes to their confrontational interpersonal style. Alternatively, or additionally, the patient may be engaged in a difficult relationship that precipitates rebelliousness or that provokes anger. One approach is to take a low-key approach to the patient, refusing to become engaged with the rebellious behavior. Often, such patients will settle down when they perceive that the therapist is not hostile and can be trusted. If further education and persuasion do not help to ameliorate this behavior, it will be necessary for you to directly confront the behavior with the patient. At this point, it may be useful to briefly explore the nature of the patient's current interpersonal situation. You can then point out the patient's pattern of repeatedly challenging you, note how this behavior is also evidenced in her everyday life, and comment on how this behavior retards progress in therapy. Finally, you may have to set limits on the patient's behavior.

The Patient with Binge-Eating Disorder

The main feature of the program for the patient with binge-eating disorder is a sensible exercise program, which should be monitored and extended. Begin also to point out items on the patient's completed Daily Food Records, indicating fatty foods that might be reduced. These changes should be introduced gradually.

Time	Food and Liquid Consumed	Location	Binge?	Exercise	Comments
7:00 a.m.	Grapenuts, non-fat milk 1 banana 2 cups coffee			15-min. walk before breakfast	breakfast
9:00 a.m.	wheat toast, honey, 1 slice				snack
10:30 a.m.	pumpkin pie 6" round	farmer's market	Binge		
11:15 a.m.	Veggie burger, lettuce, tomato dark bread bun iced tea				
11:45 a.m.	popcorn Diet Coke 8 oz.				
2:00 p.m.	turkey sandwich, whole wheat bread cranberry sauce coffee with cream				
6:00 p.m.	cinnamon roll (whole wheat with honey)				
8:00 p.m.	tortilla (baked) bean dip (non-fat) Diet Coke				

Figure 7.2

Example of Completed Session 4 Daily Food Record for Binge-Eating Patient

A sample Daily Food Record for a patient with binge-eating disorder is shown in Figure 7.2. This patient has frequent and disorganized eating episodes throughout the day. In this case, encourage the patient to start eating by the clock, with three planned meals and two snacks per day. Planning meals and snacks for each day ahead of time is helpful for this type of patient. Take some time to help the patient plan the next day's meals and snacks and to try the procedure on one or two more occasions over the next week. Be sure to praise the patient for the 15-minute walk recorded.

Homework

✎ The patient should continue working toward a regular eating pattern of three meals and two snacks per day.

✎ Instruct the patient to continue self-monitoring using the Daily Food Record.

✎ Instruct the patient to continue to weigh herself weekly and to record her weight on the Daily Food Record.

✎ Direct the binge-eating patient to continue with the agreed-upon exercise routine.

✎ Have the patient read chapter 5 of the workbook and complete the self-assessment.

Chapter 8   *Remainder of Phase 1: Sessions 5–9*

(Corresponds to chapter 6 of the workbook)

The length of this first and most important phase of treatment varies among patients. Some can accomplish this phase in two or three sessions, whereas some may take more than 10. The primary focus of this phase continues to be on restructuring the pattern of eating, helping the patient move toward a regular pattern of eating by the clock. In addition, some restructuring of the eating episodes themselves may be necessary. For example, the record shown in Chapter 6 (Figure 6.1) was of a patient whose breakfast consisted of only a latte coffee; for dinner she ate only popcorn and coffee. Such patients need to be engaged in a discussion about the type of breakfast and dinner they might be able to eat, increasing both the variety of foods in these meals and the caloric content. During this phase of treatment, it is not necessary to incorporate feared foods into the diet, but the patient should begin to add non-feared foods so that there is a clear distinction between meals and snacks. As the sessions continue, encourage the patient to gradually increase portion sizes to avoid the sensations of hunger that many bulimics report in the context column of the food diary.

An example of a therapist's agenda for Session 7 of treatment follows:

> This is Session number 7, March 19, with Susan. Plan for session today is to continue to work with the patient on eating at regular intervals. The homework for last time was having the patient come up with simple meals she can make herself. She has the expectation that she needs to make homemade meals from scratch for every meal. We talked about a strategy for making up more simple meals she can make in a short amount of time so that it will not be so overwhelming. The other homework assignment was to commit to some specific times of eating on the week-

ends, which seems to be a difficult time for her. We'll want to tackle feelings of fullness, which keep her from eating regularly, and trying to think through with her some alternative behaviors she can engage in after eating so she doesn't focus on fullness and discomfort.

The sample Daily Food Record shown in Figure 8.1 is an example of the early restructuring of meals of the highly restricted bulimic patient; her record from Session 2 was shown in Chapter 5 (Figure 5.1). This record is from Session 3, where she is beginning to regularize her eating pattern with three daily meals, although they are still extremely restricted. A suitable prescription for this patient would be to add a snack mid-morning and to begin to differentiate meals from snacks by adding more food items to the meals. This patient would undoubtedly be quite resistant to such notions (note that she feels in control, having lost 2 lbs) but should be encouraged to take risks in changing her behavior because such changes are essential to recovery. Reference to the cognitive-behavioral model may also be useful in demonstrating the effects of restrictive dieting.

A quite different sample record for another bulimic patient is shown in Figure 8.2. This patient has strong similarities to patients with binge-eating disorder. As shown, this patient is beginning to organize her eating into meals and snacks. Discussion in this case would center on the need to better plan the meals and snacks during the day, with the patient and therapist jointly planning a typical Sunday's eating episodes and a typical workday's eating episodes.

Time	Food and Liquid Consumed	Location	Binge?	Purge?	Comments
9:30 a.m.	1 bowl of soup with two slices of bread	kitchen			Feel in control, lost 2lbs
2:00 p.m.	tuna sandwich, coffee				
3:30 p.m.	Half power bar				
6:30 p.m.	chocolate chip cookies with coffee				

Figure 8.1

Example of Completed Daily Food Record for Highly Restricted Bulimic Patient

Time	Food and Liquid Consumed	Location	Binge?	Purge?	Comments
8:30 a.m.	coffee w/2 teaspoons non-fat milk & a little bit of hot chocolate mix Non-fat Yogurt – 8 oz. 1 cup Rice Chex cereal				
10:30 a.m.	1 apple, more coffee	at desk			hungry, wanted something to eat
11:10 a.m.	2 rice cakes	at desk			kind of hungry
1:00 p.m.	a little less than 1 pint chicken and rice soup from Chinese food restaurant 1 rice cake 1/2 artichoke 2 Diet Cokes (24 oz. total)	at desk			Lunchtime, hungry Didn't like seeing oil in soup. Tried to eat around it. That's why I didn't eat it all. Still feel a little hungry and still feeling down.
1:40 p.m.	2 Hershey's kisses	at desk			Craving chocolate
1:50 p.m.	1 oz peanut M&M's (about 14)	at desk			Thought about bingeing or throwing them up but tried to talk out that it was okay. I'm feeling like I may binge later today. I'm tired.
3:00 p.m.	1 medium apple	at desk			think I might be hungry
8:50 p.m.	2 large pieces apple pie, 1 slice cake		Binge	vomited	Still want to eat another piece and ended up eating it, deciding I would throw up after having B-day Pie & Cake

Figure 8.2

Example of Completed Daily Food Record for Bulimic Patient

Time	Food and Liquid Consumed	Location	Binge?	Purge?	Comments
7:00 a.m.	Grapenuts, non-fat milk 1 banana 2 cups coffee				breakfast
9:00 a.m.	wheat toast, honey, 1 slice				snack
12:00 p.m.	turkey sandwich, whole wheat bread cranberry sauce coffee/cream				lunch
4:00 p.m.	Toast with jam				snack
8:00 p.m.	1 cup beef stew with 1 cup mashed potatoes				dinner

Figure 8.3

Example of Completed Daily Food Record for Bulimic Patient

An example of a somewhat better structured Daily Food Record from Session 8 for a patient with bulimia nervosa is shown in Figure 8.3. Here, the meals can be differentiated from snacks, and the patient is eating three meals and two snacks regularly.

Meal Planning

Although many patients with bulimia nervosa or binge-eating disorder are able to restructure their eating patterns with little specific assistance, others need to learn to plan their eating episodes at specific times, often with different plans for different days of the week, for example, workdays, weekends, and any days in which the patient's schedule varies from the norm. To help the patient plan the timing of eating episodes and the content of meals and snacks, you must be familiar with the details of the patient's daily schedule. This makes it easier for you to help the patient assess the feasibility of any proposed changes. Explain to the patient that all changes are experimental and will be refined as their success or failure becomes apparent. Once an overall plan has been devised, encourage the patient to follow it. This may necessitate a stepwise approach wherein the patient uses the plan one or two days each week at first and then gradually increases the frequency. Other patients may be able to institute such plans more quickly. If a plan has been agreed upon, incorporate it into the patient's homework. Be sure to review the patient's progress in implementing the plan when you review homework.

Eating Style

An examination of the patient's eating style may be useful during this phase of treatment. Introduce the topic by reviewing the patient's comments from the completed Daily Food Records. For example, a patient may note that she ate ice cream while standing up. Further questions may reveal that she simply took the package out of the refrigerator and began to eat directly from it. This might lead to an examination of the manner and place in which all snacks and meals are consumed, with the rationale that paying attention to the context of eating may enhance self-control. Patients will often eat breakfast or snacks in the car, may binge under specific circumstances, or may eat standing up in the kitchen, watching television, and so on. Explain that by eating in a variety of places or in particular ways, those places become cues to eat. For example, if a patient eats in the car, simply getting into the car may precipitate an urge to eat. The aim is to reduce the number of places in which food is consumed, working toward limiting eating to a few places. Meals should be consumed sitting down at a table that has been laid for a meal. This topic fits well with the introduction of meal planning.

Duration and Outcome of Phase 1

As noted earlier, patients who decrease their purging by 70% by Session 6 of treatment are very likely to recover by the end of treatment or earlier. Those who do not show this pattern are far less likely to recover. At this point in treatment, it is important to explore the reasons for less than adequate progress on the patient's part. Consider the possibility that treatment should be changed or augmented.

A similar rate of improvement in binge eating should be expected for patients with binge-eating disorder. In addition to maintaining a regular pattern of meals and snacks, such patients should also be cutting down slowly on high-calorie foods, eating more appropriate foods at each meal (no leftover cake or desserts for breakfast), and participating in a regular exercise program.

Homework

✎ The patient should continue all aspects of the program (keeping Daily Food Records, working toward a regular pattern of eating, weighing herself weekly, and engaging in pleasurable alternative activities).

✎ When you are ready to move the patient into Phase 2 of treatment, have her read chapter 6 of the workbook. Direct the patient's attention to the Summary of Progress worksheets in the chapter. These exercises form the basis for the evaluation of progress in Phase 2 of treatment.

Chapter 9   *Assessing Progress*

Patient Problems

If patients have not shown an approximately 70% decline in binge eating and purging, you should first review the patient's self-monitoring records. Has the patient made progress toward the main goals of Phase 1, namely, regularizing the eating pattern and lessening overall dietary restriction? The answer to this question will highlight residual problems the patient has had in achieving these goals. Discuss these problems with the patient to find solutions. If the patient has not made suitable progress, consider the problem areas outlined later in the chapter. It should be noted, however, that we do not recommend combining another psychotherapeutic approach with cognitive-behavioral therapy. If you decide that continuing cognitive-behavioral therapy is not appropriate, then we recommend that you change the treatment approach entirely. Adding another form of psychotherapeutic treatment to cognitive-behavioral therapy blurs the focus of treatment and weakens both its effectiveness and that of the other psychotherapy.

Controlled-treatment studies of cognitive-behavioral therapy for bulimia nervosa and binge-eating disorder suggest that up to 25% of participants will drop out of therapy. Most of these dropouts occur during the first few sessions of treatment and many of them involve changes in the patient's life circumstances incompatible with the continuation of therapy (e.g., a change of jobs, financial problems, and transportation difficulties). Some of these problems—particularly whether or not patients are being realistic about the time and effort involved in the treatment—can be avoided through careful assessment of the patient's motivation before beginning treatment.

A personality disorder, such as marked impulsivity, or major interpersonal problems may also lead the patient to drop out. If such problems are identified early in treatment (and preferably before treatment begins) the therapist may decide to use an alternative approach to treatment, such as interpersonal therapy adapted for bulimia nervosa.

Apart from dropping out, the following are the main problem areas for patients who do not do well in therapy:

1. In a patient with a past history of anorexia nervosa and who continues to have strong fears of weight gain severe dietary restriction often occurs.

2. Interpersonal problems, which interfere with the course of therapy or with the patient–therapist relationship, negatively affect CBT. For example, a patient locked in a struggle with a parent while making the transition to independence may demonstrate similar behavior toward the therapist, perhaps challenging the CBT model, showing poor compliance with self-monitoring, and so on. If a straightforward confrontation concerning this issue does not ameliorate the problem, then a switch to interpersonal therapy may be desirable.

3. Another problem that may arise during the first phase of treatment is the emergence of, or deepening of, depressive symptomatology, or less frequently, the emergence or aggravation of an anxiety disorder such as panic disorder, since both these disorders demonstrate high rates of comorbidity with eating disorders. Medication treatment for both conditions may allow you to resume cognitive-behavioral therapy once the symptoms have abated.

Poor Compliance

Chapter 7 outlined several areas underlying poor compliance. In the case of patients who are not improving with cognitive-behavioral therapy, the therapist should revisit these potential problems. If the patient presents with one of these problems, you should attempt to help the patient resolve it. This may mean pointing out the lack of progress to the patient, clearly identifying the compliance problem, putting pressure on the patient to change the behavior, and pointing out that without such changes treatment is unlikely to be successful. However, before pressuring the patient to change, it is useful to attempt to identify the barriers that the patient has encountered in attempting to change the behavior. If such barriers, for example, faulty cognitions or difficult life circumstances, are identified, then these barriers can become the focus of treatment.

Frequently Encountered Therapist Problems

Not all the problems encountered in therapy stem from the patient. The therapist may also contribute to the difficulties. Perhaps the most frequent problem is failing to adhere to the structure of the sessions. Session structure is integral to successful treatment, and sessions should be structured as follows: After greeting the patient and making a general inquiry about how things have gone since the last session, review the patient's completed Daily Food Records and any other homework assigned at the last session. Then, set the session agenda and work through each of the session topics in detail. Follow this with a brief review of what has been achieved thus far. Close each session by assigning homework. Sessions that are not structured in this manner tend to become disorganized and feel unsatisfactory to both therapist and patient. In addition, less useful work is accomplished in the poorly structured session.

A second problem that may arise is that the therapist does not focus on the main aim of the initial sessions, namely, establishing a pattern of regular eating. There are a number of reasons for such a lack of focus. For example, the therapist may structure the session poorly and begin with a detailed discussion of the first session topic instead of reviewing the patient's completed homework. This tendency can be avoided by adhering to the session structure and developing an agenda for the session. The first issue may or may not appear on the agenda. Very often, such issues are not found to be relevant once one sees the larger picture. Similarly, therapists may get sidetracked when the patient presents a life problem in the session and the therapist decides to investigate the issue further. You should listen to the patient's problem empathetically but then quickly return to the main focus of the session. Tell the patient that such problems will be handled later in therapy, when you examine up-setting life events that trigger binge eating. For the moment, however, the focus should be on regaining control of eating by instituting a pattern of regular eating.

A further problem is focusing too early on the content of what the patient eats rather than on the patterning of meals and snacks. Although it is important for both the patient with bulimia nervosa and the patient with binge-eating disorder to eventually consider the introduction of feared and avoided foods, and for the overweight bulimic and the patient with binge-eating disorder to work toward a healthy diet, it is first necessary to help patients structure their eating pattern. Once the patient accomplishes this goal and binge eating is reduced, meal content can be addressed. Another therapist problem, caused in part by the more educative early sessions and the need for the therapist to be active, is to allow the patient to become too passive in the therapy session. Wherever possible, patients should be made to do the work. For example, rather than the therapist's taking the lead in reviewing the cognitive-behavioral model, the therapist might ask the patient how they see their problem fitting into the model. This will necessitate the patient's reviewing the model, aided where necessary by the therapist.

A further therapist problem is that of extending a session when the patient is late. You should always resist such an impulse. Of course, it is necessary to examine the patient's reason for being late and to problem solve so as to avoid a repetition of the behavior. However, the consequence of lateness should be a shorter session, which brings home to the patient the importance of being on time and of making the most of this opportunity to overcome the eating disorder.

Alternatives to CBT

If there has been little progress in reducing binge eating and purging, particularly if there is also little change in restructuring the pattern of eating and an increase in caloric restriction, then it is unlikely that cognitive-behavioral therapy will help this patient. Unfortunately, controlled-treatment research has not yet advanced to the point where we can give sound advice to therapists as to how to proceed in such cases;

that is, second-level treatments for patients who have made little progress in the first phase of CBT have not been addressed systematically. The following is an outline of the available options.

Add Antidepressant Medication

As noted in Chapter 1, antidepressants, both the tricyclic (e.g., imipramine, desipramine) compounds and the selective serotonin reuptake inhibitors (e.g., fluoxetine), are more effective than placebo in treating bulimia nervosa and binge-eating disorder. At this point, fluoxetine is the only antidepressant medication approved by the FDA for the treatment of bulimia nervosa. Therefore, one option is to add an antidepressant to cognitive-behavioral therapy. The tricyclic antidepressants are effective in the usual antidepressant dose, whereas fluoxetine is most effective at a daily dose of 60 mg. As noted earlier, another indication for the addition of an antidepressant is the emergence or worsening of a major depression or the emergence of panic attacks. Such symptoms, particularly depression, may interfere with treatment, and their alleviation may allow cognitive-behavioral therapy to proceed more smoothly.

Change to Interpersonal Therapy

For patients whose interpersonal problems appear to be interfering with progress and for whom interpersonal problems form a major source of triggers for binge eating, it may be reasonable to change the therapeutic procedure to interpersonal therapy in its adaptation to eating disorders (see Chapter 1). This allows for exploration of the relationship between interpersonal problems and the eating disorder and for the resolution of such problems. IPT may be particularly appropriate for patients with transient negative moods that are improved when the patient binges. In such cases, the binges may be too reinforcing for the patient to give up without attention to the sources of the negative moods. As noted in Chapter 1, IPT appears to be as effective as cognitive-behavioral therapy in treating binge-eating disorder, whereas it is not as effective in bulimia nervosa at the end of treatment but is as effective some months later.

If the patient is making reasonable progress, as indicated by an adequate decline in purging accompanied by appropriate changes in the sequencing of eating episodes, treatment can move seamlessly into the second phase. The aim of treatment in the second phase is first to address other forms of dieting, such as caloric restriction, avoidance of feared foods, and quasi-vegetarianism, and second, to address binge-eating triggers. These triggers include feared foods, faulty thinking, rigid food rules, negative affect, interpersonal conflicts that prompt negative emotions, and weight and shape concerns. In the last few sessions, the patient has probably been listing on the self-monitoring form the circumstances in which binge eating has occurred. The therapist should have been noting these circumstances for future reference because they often indicate binge triggers. If the patient has not been listing such circumstances, they should now be encouraged to do so. It may be useful at this point for the therapist to explore with the patient the particular events, internal or external, that trigger binge eating. This will allow the therapist and patient to address the most salient issues in the second phase of treatment.

Treatment Phase 2: Identifying Binge Triggers

Chapter 10 *Introduction to Phase 2*

The transition from the first to the second phase of therapy should be quite smooth because it follows naturally from the aims of the first phase of treatment. The transition usually occurs somewhere between Sessions 6 and 10 but may occur earlier for patients who make rapid progress toward the goals of Phase 1. Remember, Phase 1 goals for the patient with binge-eating disorder also include establishing a regular exercise program, decreasing the consumption of high-calorie foods, and adopting a heart-healthy diet. The second phase of treatment usually ends some three sessions before therapy is scheduled to terminate. A primary aim of the second phase of treatment is to continue to monitor, and to extend if necessary, progress toward, or maintenance of, a regular eating pattern (and for the patient with binge-eating disorder, a regular exercise program and continued decrease in the consumption of high-calorie foods). Do not lose sight of this aim, even when dealing with new issues in the next two phases of therapy. The aim of Phase 2 is to help the patient delineate the nature and extent of feared and avoided foods, and to gradually reintroduce some of these foods into the diet. In addition to continuing to address dietary triggers for binge eating (e.g., dietary restriction and avoidance of various types of food), the therapist should assess other types of binge triggers the patient is experiencing (e.g., breaking a food or dietary rule, worrying about weight and shape, and having a negative effect) so as to prioritize the issues to be addressed.

Although the various procedures are presented in a particular sequence in this manual, you may wish to introduce them in a different sequence, or with a different emphasis, depending on the patient's specific problems. Not all the issues may need to be addressed, leaving time for a more in-depth approach to other problems.

Following the introduction of feared foods, the next problem behavior to explore is the patient's attitudes and behaviors regarding weight and shape. Problems with weight and shape are an integral aspect of bulimia nervosa and should be addressed fairly early in the second phase of treatment. Although patients with BED also have increased concerns about weight and shape, this issue is not as important for these patients, and other issues, especially interpersonal issues, may need to be explored more urgently. Alternatively, in the patient with bulimia nervosa, negative affect and interpersonal issues are addressed only when they form a primary aspect of the patient's problem.

The next procedure delineates the patient's erroneous beliefs about food, shape, and weight, and challenges such beliefs through formal cognitive restructuring, with the patient practicing the use of the procedure between sessions. As for problem solving, the patient should use the Cognitive-Restructuring worksheet in the workbook to write down examples of using problem solving during the week. Finally, it should be noted that the session structure for this phase remains unchanged; you will first examine Daily Food Records and check on specific homework assignments; then outline the agenda, based on this examination and the progress of therapy; work through the agenda; recap the session; and assign homework. However, the content of sessions will change as different aspects of the problem are addressed.

Because Phase 2 skills are not tied to particular sessions (you may wish to devote multiple sessions to certain skills), chapters in this section of the therapist guide do not include session outlines. However, you should continue to follow the standard agenda for Phase 2 sessions, which includes conducting a homework review at the start of every meeting and assigning a homework exercise at the end.

Chapter 11   *Feared and Avoided Foods*

(Corresponds to chapters 7 and 8 of the workbook)

Feared and Avoided Foods

An aspect of dietary restriction not addressed in Phase 1 of treatment is the extent to which the patient avoids feared foods. Feared and avoided foods often trigger binge eating, are eaten during binges, and may be regarded by the patient as fattening, "bad," high in calories, or high in fat content. Almost certainly, the patient will have a rule concerning such foods; for example, because they are "bad" and fattening, they should never be eaten. The patient's self-monitoring records will usually reveal, by their absence, some of the foods she is avoiding, allowing you to put the issue of feared foods on the agenda and to encourage her to talk about the nature and extent of foods she fears or has placed on the "bad foods" list. Explore the history of the patient's food avoidances, the nature of the avoidance, and the reasons for avoidance. It may be useful at this point to educate the patient regarding the issue of avoiding foods. First, explain that avoidance of anything that is feared will strengthen the fear. The only way to overcome a problem is to face it. Second, because many, if not all, of the feared foods are inherently enjoyable, by avoiding such foods, individuals are setting themselves up to feel deprived and are thereby increasing the attractiveness of these foods. This often ends with the individual buying such foods and bingeing on them.

There are two steps to conquering the fear of these foods. The first is to have the patient identify the range of foods she currently avoids. One way to achieve this aim is to have the patient visit a supermarket with a pencil and notebook and write down all foods that she regularly avoids, that cause anxiety, or that are "forbidden." For homework, instruct the patient to use the Feared and Problem Foods List in the workbook to cat-

Category 1 (least feared)	Category 2	Category 3	Category 4 (most feared)
Turkey	Pasta	Ice cream, one serving	Cheese
Veal	Sushi	Doughnuts	Tempura
Beef (fresh)	Noodles	Candy bars	Peanut Butter
Ham	Rice	Raisins	Fudge
Hamburger lean	White Bread	Pies	Pizza
Yogurt	Pancakes	Pudding	Cakes with frosting
Lettuce, green beans	Muffins	Mousse	Potato chips
Chicken	Bagels	Nuts	Chocolates, chocolate bars
Potatoes	Trail mix	Quiche	Brownies
Tofu	Hummus	Beef jerky in large bags	Cookies with frosting
Soup—most any kind		Donuts	French fries
Eggs		Any bakery items	Pints of ice cream
Milk			Fig Newtons

Figure 11.1

Example of Completed Feared and Problem Foods List

egorize these foods, putting the least feared in Category 1, and the most feared in Category 4. A sample completed list is shown in Figure 11.1.

The second step to overcoming a fear of certain foods is to have the patient begin to introduce small quantities of feared foods into her everyday diet. This work can be done in the next session. The first foods to be introduced should be from the least feared category (Category 1), and the patient should be encouraged to introduce one or two of these foods into her diet over the next week. Monitor the patient's progress toward this goal, and work with her to introduce new food items in subsequent weeks. Hence, the reintroduction of feared foods becomes a new theme running through several sessions of the second phase of treatment, with the principal aim of continuing to reduce dietary restriction.

It is important to let patients know that they are not expected to eat their feared foods regularly. Rather, they should no longer deprive themselves of these foods or regard them fearfully but should instead consume them at appropriate times within the appropriate meal or snack. Some patients become afraid that consuming such foods will lead to weight gain. This is irrational because eating small or even moderate amounts of a particular food will not influence weight. Moreover, patients have to begin to trust their bodies to regulate their food intake.

The Patient with Binge-Eating Disorder

The patient with binge-eating disorder may or may not agree about the existence of feared foods because many of these patients eat such foods at mealtimes. In such cases, the supermarket list should include both feared foods (if any) and high-calorie foods that the patient eats (perhaps with guilt or anxiety). The aim here is to encourage the consumption of feared foods (in the bulimic) and to gradually decrease the inappropriate eating of high-calorie foods (in the binge eater).

Homework

✎ The patient should continue all aspects of the program (keeping Daily Food Records, working toward a regular pattern of eating, weighing herself weekly, and engaging in pleasurable alternative activities).

✎ Instruct the patient to create a list of feared foods, using the Feared and Problem Foods List in the workbook

✎ Ask patient to begin incorporating feared foods into her everyday diet and track her progress toward this goal, using the Daily Food Record

✎ Have patient read chapter 7 of the workbook and complete the self-assessment

✎ Have patient also read chapter 8 of the workbook and complete the chapter exercises and self-assessment

Chapter 12 *Weight and Shape Concerns*

(Corresponds to chapter 9 of the workbook)

Weight and Shape Concerns

An important reason patients continue to restrict their diets is concern about weight and shape. Such concerns are fueled by low self-esteem, which may stem from many different types of developmental problems. Often, bulimics have been teased about being fat or have been regarded as being overweight by their families, and so on. Moreover, in the Western world today, the social pressure to achieve a thin body shape, a shape quite impossible for most women to attain, gives rise to body dissatisfaction in many normal women. Concerns about shape and weight in the bulimic are exaggerated by exposure to ideals presented in various media. It is important to realize that it will not be possible to totally eliminate the patient's concerns about weight and shape, although it should be possible to ameliorate such concerns.

Though she may find them "normal," the patient's perceptions about her body shape are in fact usually exaggerated. There is a range of such concerns in both the patient with bulimia nervosa and the patient with binge-eating disorder, with some patients demonstrating little more than normative discontent with their bodies, whereas others demonstrate gross perceptual distortion concerning their weight and shape. Patients in the latter group are often of a thin build with a past history of anorexia nervosa.

The first step in treatment is to explore the patient's behaviors and thinking about body shape in detail. This will usually be fairly simple because the patient will have talked about some of these concerns already and is likely to spontaneously mention such concerns in the course of treatment. The main elements to explore in this assessment are:

1. What is the history of the development of weight and shape concerns in the patient?

2. What types of weight and shape concerns does the patient have? What aspects of her body concern her?

3. What type of body-checking behaviors does the patient use, and how frequently? It is important here to examine elements such as looking at her body in the mirror (what aspects of her body does she attend to?), looking at herself in shop windows, and checking on her thighs, arms, and stomach by pinching or measuring.

4. Does the patient avoid exposing her body to others? This behavior may include wearing clothes that hide parts of her body and not swimming or going to the beach because she would have to wear a bathing suit. The behavior may be so extreme as to include not allowing her spouse or lover to see her whole body naked.

5. Does the patient read fashion magazines?

6. Does the patient compare herself with others? Although such a comparison is with a real person, it is usually the idealized form of that person, with the patient always feeling that her body is much worse than the other person's.

7. Does the patient exhibit painful or obsessive thinking about shape and weight?

The behaviors revealed by these specific questions will allow the therapist to formulate a tailored approach to each patient's problems. Although patients with binge-eating disorder also demonstrate distorted thinking about weight and shape, this is usually in the context of being overweight or obese. However, the same approach to exploring their weight and shape concerns should be taken.

Addressing the patient's concerns about weight and shape may include resolving the following issues:

1. *Body checking.* Here it is important to specifically address each type of checking. However, the basic principle is to persuade the patient to stop the behavior completely. You may want to question the patient as to how she feels after she has checked her body.

Usually the patient will report that she feels anxious, disturbed, or unhappy. You can point out to the patient that checking her body causes her to feel either only momentarily better about herself or else worse. This may motivate the patient to begin to abandon checking, abruptly or in stages. Self-monitoring exercises might include noting in the comments column of the Daily Food Record the number of times she checks her body.

2. *Avoidance.* Here you will need to address each patient's specific behaviors. However, the principle remains the same: increasing exposure of one's body to others, within normal limits. This will probably necessitate gradually shaping more appropriate behaviors.

3. *Fashion magazines.* Discuss with the patient fashion models and the practicality of anyone's achieving or maintaining the figure these models portray. The patient is probably upset when she compares her own body to those of models. You can point out that such upset can be avoided by not reading fashion magazines. (One patient had collected a garage full of such magazines and was eventually persuaded to throw them out, much to her eventual relief.)

4. *Comparison to others.* As noted above, bulimic patients usually idealize others. Have the patient critically examine others in, for example, a shopping center. Patients usually discover that no one of their own age has a perfect body.

5. *Unrealistic thinking about shape and weight.* You might address these concerns as in the example below. That is, encourage the patient to challenge her problematic thoughts.

Case Vignette

In the following example, T represents the therapist and P represents the patient.

P: I purged because I was convinced that if I kept my dinner down, I would definitely gain weight, especially since I have been eating more regular meals and snacks and I have already gained 2 lbs since starting treatment. I feel like the weight gain is just going to continue endlessly.

T: I hear some distortions there. First, what did you eat for dinner that made you so confident of an automatic, continuous weight gain?

P: Well, I was out for dinner with friends. I had half a salad, half of my serving of pasta, one glass of wine, and two pieces of French bread, and I shared a dessert with a friend. I just felt like because I've already gained a few pounds, keeping this dinner down would contribute to my weight's continuing to go up.

T: The dinner sounds pretty normal to me. But I'm hearing that you're afraid you're going to keep gaining weight beyond the 2 lbs you've put on, and you thought this dinner would contribute to that process. I'm wondering if it's possible that you are exaggerating the effects on your weight of keeping down the dinner and are translating a 2-lb gain into a continuous trend upward in your weight.

P: Well, it's possible, but I feel like it's the real truth, that I will continue to gain weight if I keep food like that down on a more regular basis.

T: Since you are open to the possibility that there is some distortion in your thoughts about the food and its potential to cause weight gain, how about we use the method to challenge problem thoughts to look at the evidence on both sides? You know the method; let's start with the first step, identifying the underlying problem thought, and take it from there.

P: OK, the first step, the underlying problem thought, is that "if I keep my dinner down, I'll continue to gain weight beyond the initial 2 lbs." Step 2, the evidence to support, is that I did eat more fat than usual, the pasta had cream sauce on it, and the dessert was a rich chocolate cake. And I felt really full after.

T: Is "feeling full" objective evidence that we can use here to support your thought?

P: Well, I guess not, but I was really full, and it made me feel as if I had eaten too much and would gain weight.

T: That may be yet another problem thought for us to address in a future session. But for right now, let's stick with this one. Is there any more objective evidence to support your belief that you'd gain weight by keeping your dinner down?

P: Yeah, there is. I have gained 2 lbs already in the first several weeks of treatment, maybe because I have begun to eat more regularly. So, that is evidence, along with the fact that it was a higher calorie dinner than usual. So, I guess we go to the other side now, evidence to refute or cast doubt on my thought. Um, the truth is, I hadn't eaten much that whole day. I had exercised quite a bit so probably really needed the calories that I took in at dinner. Also, I really did stick with half portions of everything, so I took home leftovers to have for lunch the next day. I ate much less than everyone else. And I'm sure they didn't gain weight after eating their food. I've eaten like this before without gaining weight. And I know based on that model that when I keep good meals like this down, I binge less frequently, so I'm really taking in fewer calories. I also know that the 2-lb gain might be just an arbitrary blip upward. I only noticed it during the last weigh-in, and you shouldn't consider a weight gain to be significant until you see it for four weeks. It might just be water weight or something. So there is no real reason to think that I would necessarily have gained weight from that dinner or that an uncontrollable gain is already under way.

T: Is there enough evidence to draw a reasoned conclusion then?

P: Yeah, I guess I would say that, first off, even though I've "gained" 2 lbs, that might be an arbitrary gain because it occurred only during one week's weigh-in. So, certainly, keeping down one dinner, which was really moderately sized if I think about, would do little as far as contributing to the gain. If anything, it would have just prevented me from binge eating again, and that is what leads to weight gain more quickly, because of all the calories. So, I guess I'd say that I'm probably not on an upward trend with my weight, and certainly the dinner would not have contributed to an ongoing weight gain.

Other approaches to the problem of weight gain during therapy might include analyzing the pros and cons of gaining a few pounds versus the costs of having the continuing symptoms of bulimia nervosa. Some patients, particularly those with high dietary restraint and low weight, may need to be encouraged to buy larger clothes as they gain a few pounds so that the tightness of their clothing does not continually set off worries about weight and shape. For the patient with binge-eating disorder, or the overweight bulimic, it is still reasonable to analyze the costs and benefits of ceasing dietary restriction. However, such patients should develop a healthy lifestyle with a sensible exercise regimen and sensible alterations in food choices rather than dietary restriction that leads to deprivation and hunger.

Common Types of Body-Image Concerns and Suggested Interventions

Overvaluation of a Slim Figure

The cultural pressure to be thin can sometimes be used to advantage with the bulimic patient. You can point out that different cultures at different times have had different ideals concerning weight and shape. In many cultures (including the Western world, until recently), a more rounded, fuller body was regarded as ideal and more feminine. It might be pointed out that, biologically, this is a more realistic expectation. Patients might be questioned as to whether or not they want to buy in to inappropriate cultural expectations. In addition, patients might be prompted to think more broadly about their good points, outside of weight and shape, and to begin to value such aspects more highly and to spend more effort developing these traits. Finally, for homework, patients might be told to observe other women's figures more realistically, whether at shopping centers or at the health club. They will undoubtedly find that women come in many shapes and sizes and that, in this context, their own concerns about weight and shape may be exaggerated.

Amplification of Ingrained Beliefs About Being Fat

As noted earlier in this chapter, many bulimics will have had a number of hurtful experiences concerning weight and shape, often over a considerable period of time, leading to a core belief that they are fat and unattractive. Such beliefs can be activated by negative mood stemming from a variety of causes. An example follows.

Case Vignette

In the following example, T represents the therapist and P represents the patient.

P: I felt like I might binge on Saturday. I went shopping and started trying on clothes and got a horrible case of feeling fat and ugly.

T: What was going on at the time?

P: Nothing. It was just that I looked in the mirror after trying on some pants, and I really did look horrible, fat, and stocky.

T: Well, did those feelings begin only after you tried on the pants, or is it possible that you began your self-criticism some time before?

P: I get that way every time I shop. But, come to think of it, I tend to shop when I have nothing else planned, usually on a weekend, when I'm getting lonely and slipping into a bad mood. So, maybe it actually started even before I left home, before I got to the store and tried on the pants.

T: What I'm hearing is that you had a low mood because you had nothing planned on the weekend and were feeling lonely. You decided to go shopping to try to rouse yourself from this bad mood but ended up feeling even worse, focusing all the negative energy on criticisms of your body shape. Is it possible that you displaced some of the other, more complicated feelings, feeling down and lonely and not having plans, onto that familiar theme involving the concerns about your body weight and shape?

P: It is possible, but I really did look fat. But I guess maybe there was more going on. And if I knew that and was able to step back a bit from my obsession with my body, I wouldn't have felt as tempted to do more binge eating and purging. I would have understood that my feelings were not really about the weight issue. And that would have maybe gotten me started on figuring out solutions for the real problems, like how to spend my time on weekends.

As discussed previously, using one or more of these therapeutic strategies can do much to ameliorate the disturbed feelings that bulimics, including those patients with binge-eating disorder, have concerning their weight and shape. However, it is probably inevitable that the patient will continue to be somewhat preoccupied with weight and shape. Nonetheless, by addressing this issue in the later stages of therapy, the patient can be made more aware of the unrealistic nature of such beliefs and of the role that they may play in leading to the urge to binge.

Homework

✎ The patient should continue all aspects of the program (keeping Daily Food Records, working toward a regular pattern of eating, weighing herself weekly, engaging in pleasurable alternative activities, and incorporating feared foods into her diet).

✎ Have the patient read chapter 9 of the workbook and complete the chapter exercises and self-assessment quiz.

Chapter 13 *Faulty Thinking*

(Corresponds to chapters 10 and 11 of the workbook)

Distorted Thinking

Distorted thinking about a variety of issues is a common binge-eating trigger. Most patients are not aware of the thoughts that lead to binge eating and feel instead that the whole process is automatic and out of their control. Encourage the patient to explore and note the nature of her thinking that leads to binge eating. It is also helpful to educate the patient about her thought processes, pointing out that although it may not seem to be the case, she has a considerable degree of control over her thoughts. She should be able to detect thoughts that lead to binges and, with your help, learn to challenge and correct faulty thinking. When a patient begins to explore her thinking, she may confuse feelings with thoughts, making it necessary for you to help her make the distinction. At the same time, the patient should learn to pay attention to thoughts linked to strong feelings because these salient "thought–feelings" may represent "hot" cognitions and seem likely to trigger binge eating. As the patient begins to identify the thoughts that trigger binge eating, encourage her to identify the core aspect of the thought. Then teach the patient the method of evaluating the reality of the particular thought, with the aim of changing such thinking and the behavior that results.

Types of Distorted Thinking

Distorted thinking usually falls into one of five categories, although the categories overlap.

1. *Using all-or-nothing thinking.* This type of thinking is particularly common in bulimics, both in bulimia nervosa and in binge-eating

disorder. Extreme thoughts such as, "Either I am on a diet or I am out of control" are typical. This type of thinking is often combined with perfectionism, with the patient setting overly high standards (e.g., "Unless I come in every week with no binge episodes I am a failure").

2. *Overgeneralizing.* This distortion consists of making an erroneous conclusion about general performance, or a series of unrelated events, based on a single negative experience; for example, "I gained 2 lbs this week, so I know I will keep gaining weight at that rate," or "I binged on potato chips once, so I must never again eat potato chips." Such thinking underlies the rigid rules governing food consumption that many bulimics elaborate.

3. *Magnifying negatives and minimizing positives.* This is also a very common distortion bulimics engage in and one that the therapist should be alert to. The patient may come to the session reporting that she had a terrible week. However, when you examine the food records, it turns out that the patient binged only once during the week, that the binge was subjective, and that she did not purge. Here the patient is ignoring positive behaviors and focusing only on negative ones. A similar example might be a patient who comes in very upset because someone made a derogatory remark about her appearance. It turns out that the remark was made by a girlfriend who is jealous of her and that there were several times when others complimented her appearance that same week. The therapist should be alert to this type of behavior during all phases of cognitive-behavioral therapy. You can help the patient overcome selective distortion by exploring the positive gains and good experiences she has had since the last session.

4. *Catastrophizing.* Here the patient overestimates the negative consequences of a particular event. "If I gain 5 lbs, everyone will notice. They will think that I am unattractive, and I will be rejected." Again, this distortion is frequently encountered in the bulimic.

5. *Using selective abstraction.* In this distortion, the patient bases a conclusion on isolated details while ignoring contradictory and often more salient evidence; for example, "No one talked to me at the party, so it must be because they think I'm fat and ugly."

Teach the patient the formal problem-solving method of exploring and correcting her distorted thinking, and once she has mastered the method in session, encourage her to practice the method on her own to identify and correct thoughts as they occur. At first she might want to delineate one or two such thoughts during the week between sessions, writing out the formal method on the back of the self-monitoring sheets. The process occurs in four steps.

A sample patient–therapist dialogue illustrates each of the steps that follows.

Step 1: Identify the Problem Thought

T: Did you notice any situations leading to binge episodes or to urges to binge in the past week that involve problem thoughts?

P: Well, I binged after skiing one day. I was upset because I went skiing and people were nicer to my girlfriend than they were to me, and I was sure it was because she is thinner and prettier than I am.

T: I'm hearing some faulty reasoning here. Let's work to distill the essence of the underlying problem thought.

P: My friend is prettier than I am, so that means that people like her more and like me less, and she's thinner. So, I guess the underlying problem thought is that people don't like me because I'm fat and ugly. *(At this point the therapist should have the patient write down the problem thought on a sheet of paper.)*

Step 2: Evidence to Support the Thought

T: What is the evidence to support the view that people don't like you because you're fat and ugly?

P: Well, I am fat and ugly.

T: Come on! I think you know that is subjective, not objective.

P: OK. Objectively, my friend is more attractive than I am.

T: Let's accept that for now and write it down.

P: I was not looking my best that day.

T: Again a stretch, but we'll accept that for now. *(Have patient write the thought down.)* Are there others?

P: More people talked to her than to me.

T: OK. Let's go with those.

Step 3: Evidence to Refute

T: What about the other side of it? What is the evidence you can use to cast doubts on your views?

P: I know that even though I feel fat, objectively my weight is in the normal range. I know that even though I feel ugly, people have told me I'm attractive. I think that when I am feeling fat and ugly, people may stay away from me because of the way I carry myself when I'm feeling that way, not because of how I look.

T: I think we just got somewhere. Why don't you write down the reasons to refute your original view? You feel fat and ugly but receive feedback that you are attractive. You feel fat, but your weight is within the normal range. When you are feeling fat and ugly you behave in a standoffish way so people shy away from you. Do I have it right?

P: Yes.

Step 4: Reasoned Conclusion Based on All the Evidence

T: So, given your evidence to support and refute, can you come up with a reasoned conclusion that counters your original problem thought?

P: I think so. It goes like this: "When I'm feeling fat and ugly it seems like people don't like me because of my looks, but really they are reacting to the way I am projecting myself because I feel unattractive. That's something I can work on."

T: OK, let's write that down. With that conclusion in mind, do you think you would have left the situation not feeling the urge to binge and purge?

P: Yes. I wouldn't have felt so depressed and lonely afterward.

T: Good. Why don't you try to identify another thought or two during the next week, and follow the method we have just used, writing it down on the Cognitive-Restructuring worksheet in your workbook? Then we can take a look at it in the next session.

It should be noted that patients vary in their ability to apply cognitive restructuring. Although many patients find this approach useful, there are some who are not comfortable with the technique and find they cannot use it. Use other procedures to deal with binge triggers when treating such patients.

Homework

✎ The patient should continue all aspects of the program (keeping Daily Food Records, working toward a regular pattern of eating, weighing herself weekly, engaging in pleasurable alternative activities, and incorporating feared foods into her diet).

✎ The binge-eating patient should continue incorporating exercise into her daily routine.

✎ If not done during Phase 1 (see Chapter 6), have the patient read chapter 10 of the workbook and complete the chapter exercises and self-assessment.

✎ Have the patient read chapter 11 of the workbook and complete the self-assessment.

Chapter 14 | *Negative Mood*

(Corresponds to chapter 12 of the workbook)

Negative Mood as a Binge Trigger

The antecedent event bulimics most frequently report as triggering binge eating is a negative mood. Such moods arise from a number of sources, including reactions to faulty thinking about food or weight and shape, failure to achieve an impossible standard, and problematic interpersonal interactions. The patient may note in the comments column of the Daily Food Record the negative mood, a derogatory comment about performance, or an interpersonal interaction leading to a binge. It is important for you to help the patient investigate the exact nature of the events leading up to the negative mood and eventually to the decision to binge eat. The best way to accomplish this is to work backward from the immediate precipitant of the binge.

Research suggests that transient negative moods have several effects. First, such moods appear to enhance the perception of loss of control over eating. Loss of control is associated with both negative affect, whether depression, anxiety, or anger, and negative cognitions, sometimes about personal performance (e.g., "I'm a failure") and sometimes about the binge episode (e.g., "I'm a pig, I'm like an animal"). The patient who can identify these types of thoughts can challenge them using the methods outlined in the previous chapter. Second, in a negative mood, patients are more likely to classify an eating episode as a binge, regardless of the amount of food eaten. Examine the patient's Daily Food Record for that particular eating episode to confirm whether or not it actually was a binge. Third, it is likely that patients overestimate the amount of food they have eaten when in a negative mood state. As we know from experiments with normal but dietary-restricted women, simply believing that they have eaten too much leads to overeating in the laboratory.

Again, you can check the patient's Daily Food Records to ascertain the basis for such perceptions. Finally, many patients, rightly or wrongly, feel that binge eating offers an escape from and relieves their negative feelings, and there is evidence that such moods do decrease in the short term in the context of binge eating.

There are several ways of approaching episodes of transient negative mood. First, faulty perceptions can be challenged using the self-monitoring records. Second, faulty cognitions can be clarified and challenged using the cognitive-restructuring technique. Third, the exact nature of the interpersonal events leading up to the binge can be detailed. If such events appear to be quite specific and often associated with binge eating, problem solving can be used to find alternative, more adaptive methods of coping with such events. For example, it may be that the patient becomes upset because her boyfriend is late for their dinner plans, and time is passing. She tries calling him, but he doesn't answer. This has two effects: She becomes angry, and then she becomes hungry. There are several ways to cope with this type of situation. The patient might consider having a snack or, if it is too late, going out for a meal by herself. She could also prepare a meal at home or go out to eat with a girlfriend.

It is also possible to take a broader approach to such interpersonal problems. Here the therapist helps the patient explore the nature of the relationship with her boyfriend, how they interact in general, and, more specifically, the details of the incident triggering the negative mood and binge eating. Having delineated the problem, the therapist can then suggest to the patient that she try new ways of interacting with her boyfriend over such incidents, and various alternative behaviors might be discussed. These new approaches to the relationship then become homework that is reviewed at the next session, when further exploratory work on the relationship may be necessary. This exploration should remain fairly tightly focused on interpersonal events that trigger binges. There is not enough time to fully explore and resolve all troublesome aspects of such relationships in the context of cognitive-behavioral therapy.

Patients should regard negative mood as a warning that they may be at risk for a binge. First, they should attempt to clarify the reasons for the negative mood and then problem solve solutions either to the negative mood or to their immediate problem of being at risk for a binge. Resolving a negative mood might include examining distorted cognitions regarding the precipitant of the mood. In addition, patients at risk for a persistent negative mood should pay careful attention to eating three meals and two snacks at regular intervals to lower the risk of binge eating.

In summary, negative affect arising from unsuccessful interpersonal interactions can be approached through cognitive restructuring or problem solving, or by using a more direct means aimed at engendering more successful interpersonal interactions. Choose the most helpful approach, based on your assessment of the situation. By this point in therapy, you will have a good deal of knowledge about the patient's interpersonal situation. This will make the task of choosing an appropriate response easier.

Homework

✎ The patient should continue all aspects of the program (keeping Daily Food Records, working toward a regular pattern of eating, weighing herself weekly, engaging in pleasurable alternative activities, and incorporating feared foods into her diet).

✎ Have the patient read chapter 12 of the workbook and complete the chapter exercises and self-assessment.

Treatment Phase 3: Maintaining Change

Chapter 15 | *Final Sessions: Relapse Prevention*

(Corresponds to chapter 13 of the workbook)

Relapse prevention is the third phase of cognitive-behavioral treatment and usually spans the final two or three sessions. Other issues, like dealing with binge triggers and tracking dietary intake to prevent and/or continue to diminish dietary restriction, should also be covered in these final sessions. The session structure remains unaltered and incorporates all the standard elements, including opening the session with a greeting and a general inquiry as to how the patient is doing, followed by reviewing homework, setting the agenda, and reviewing the main topics of the session. At the end of each session, you will assign homework. It is useful to see the patient only once every two weeks in this phase. This schedule allows the patient a longer interval in which to experience and attempt to resolve residual problems.

Relapse Prevention: Part 1

In the first session of Phase 3, ask the patient to consider what aspects of the program have been most useful in helping bring the binge eating and purging under control. Ask the patient to look forward to the weeks and months following the end of treatment and to begin to anticipate the types of problems that may lead to a lapse in binge eating and/or purging. Discuss with the patient any ideas she has for coping with lapses. The homework assignment is to develop a written plan for coping with situations that put the patient at risk for binge eating or purging; this plan increases the probability of the patient maintaining improvements.

During this discussion, clarify the difference between a lapse and a relapse. A lapse is a *brief* (i.e., comprising a few episodes, hours, or days) return to a problem behavior that seemed resolved. A *relapse* represents a return to the problem behavior for an extended period. Handling a lapse promptly can prevent a relapse. It is important for the patient not to catastrophize lapses by misperceiving them as relapses, where all the gains made in therapy have been lost. Point out that, in the last few weeks of treatment, there will be time to test methods to address some of the high-risk situations leading to ongoing binge eating. Patients should take care to identify times when they have an urge to binge eat, even if it is transient, and should attempt to identify the precipitating circumstance and what methods they used to successfully avoid binge eating.

In the second session, which addresses relapse prevention, review and discuss the patient's maintenance plan. If the patient has had difficulty finding strategies to cope with some of her high-risk situations, use the problem-solving method within the session. Similarly, if you are familiar with high-risk situations the patient may have experienced in the past, discuss them and determine whether they currently pose a high risk. Again, encourage the patient to use the methods taught in this program to cope with her high-risk situations between sessions.

During this session, inform the patient of the various options open to her after she completes this program. Such options will differ for the successful and unsuccessful patient and will therefore be discussed separately below.

The Successful Patient

The successful patient is likely to have stopped binge eating several weeks ago or may binge eat only sporadically. (Usually, these are binges of the subjective variety, i.e., small binges with a sense of loss of control.) This patient therefore likely has a good sense of the triggers for such binges and has crafted a well-developed plan for coping with such triggers. One study suggested that patients with BN who had not binged or purged for at least the final 6 weeks of treatment had the best chance of maintaining their gains. Depending on their progress, patients might be offered further consultations if they experience renewed problems with their eating disorder that they feel they cannot cope with adequately alone. Patients who continue to binge eat sporadically can be told that, if they continue to apply the methods they have learned during therapy, they have an excellent chance of continuing to see improvements over the next several months. Such patients might be offered further consultation when they feel it is needed, or, if they prefer, they might be offered regular sessions at longer intervals, for example, once a month. There is no research that illuminates the best course to take for patients who have completed cognitive-behavioral therapy; however, follow-up studies suggest that the months immediately following the completion of treatment appear to be a time of high risk for relapse.

During the course of therapy, the patient and therapist may have discovered residual problems related to the eating disorder but outside the realm of cognitive-behavioral therapy, such as interpersonal problems. In these cases, the patient and therapist might wish to address the problems in further sessions, although it should be clear to the patient that CBT treatment specifically addressed to the eating disorder has ended. Alternatively, recovery from the eating disorder might be accompanied by recognition of a comorbid problem now posing difficulties for the patient. For example, because the patient has more time to engage in behaviors outside of binge eating and purging, symptoms of a social phobia may become more apparent. In such cases, discuss the patient's options for treatment for that condition.

The Unsuccessful Patient

One hopes that unsuccessful patients will have been identified earlier in the course of treatment and an alternative or additional therapy modality put into effect with good results. For patients who continue to meet, or nearly meet, criteria for bulimia nervosa or binge-eating disorder after treatment, the options are much the same as those detailed in Chapter 1. The principal options are to add antidepressant medication, or, if it appears appropriate, to switch to interpersonal therapy for an eating disorder. It should be noted that there has been only one study of adding interpersonal therapy for patients who failed to improve with cognitive-behavioral therapy. That study involved patients with binge-eating disorder, and it was found that interpersonal therapy did not confer additional benefits for them. Hence, any advice you give the patient should be based on their particular clinical situation.

Homework

✎ Have the patient develop a final maintenance plan.

✎ Have the patient read chapter 13 of the workbook and complete the chapter exercises and self-assessment.

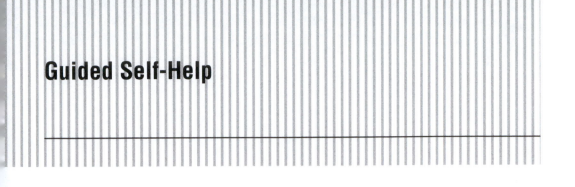

Guided Self-Help

Chapter 16 | *Therapist-Assisted Self-Help*

As noted in Chapter 1, evidence is accumulating that therapist-assisted self-help based on the CBT model is as effective as full CBT both for bulimia nervosa and for binge-eating disorder. The approach to this mode of treatment is very different from that of full CBT. First, the patient workbook forms the basis for treatment. The patient is expected to read the workbook, which for them is the principal form of treatment. The therapist should also be very familiar with the book so that patients can be referred to appropriate sections and pages, depending on the progress of treatment. Second, the number and length of sessions differ considerably from those for CBT. Therapy is more tightly focused on the patient's achieving regular eating and diminishing dieting; less attention is given to other aspects of the problem, such as interpersonal triggers and cognitive restructuring.

Therapist-assisted self-help has been conducted successfully by master's-level therapists, by nurses, and by PhD-level therapists. Nothing is known about the relative effectiveness of different levels of experience or expertise. Therapists should read both this chapter and the accompanying self-help patient workbook.

The Self-Help Workbook

The self-help workbook is divided into two parts. The first part briefly describes bulimia nervosa and binge-eating disorder, their effects on health and well-being, and the evidence for the effectiveness of cognitive-behavioral therapy, on which the workbook is based. In addition, the growing evidence for the effectiveness of therapist-assisted self-help is described. The second part of the book describes the treatment program, which is divided into several steps. These steps have been carefully sequenced and build on each other.

Treatment consists of 8–10 sessions, beginning with a 50-minute session to establish a therapeutic relationship and take an adequate history of the eating disorder. You will introduce and orient the patient to the self-help program in this session as well. Following this session, the patient will have therapy sessions once a week for the next 4 weeks. This ensures continuity of treatment for the initial sessions. After the first 4 weeks, the 25-minute sessions occur every 2 weeks, and at about 2 months, they occur at monthly intervals. The reason to space the sessions as treatment proceeds is to give patients more time to work on their problem.

Treatment Outline and Structure

Because the therapy sessions are brief, the therapist needs to be well organized. Be sure to review relevant information from this book before conducting each session. See Table 16.1 for a list of therapist guide chapters that correspond to the self-directed workbook. Review the particular information from these chapters and use it to facilitate sessions. Also review treatment notes, confirm the status of the patient at the last session, and go over completed homework with the patient. In addition, pay close attention to the patient's mastery of each skill as treatment progresses. Use this information to determine whether or not to proceed to the next step.

Session 1 Outline

- Establish a working relationship with the patient.

- Take a relatively brief history of the patient's eating disorder and present symptoms.

- Describe the method of treatment, namely, that this is a form of self-help guided by the therapist. The patient is expected to do much of the work, particularly reading the book and working to

Table 16.1 Self-Directed Workbook and Corresponding Therapist Guide Chapters

	Self-Directed Workbook		Corresponding Therapist Guide Chapter(s)
Chapter	Title	Summary	
2	Binge Eating and Purging	Description of binge eating and purging, epidemiology of BN and BED, risk factors for the disorder, and the CBT model	Chapter 1
3	Health Effects of Binge Eating and Purging	Health effects of binge eating and purging, including both physical and psychological problems as well as effects on living	Chapter 2
4	Treatments for Binge Eating and Purging	Description of evidence-based treatments for BN and BED including medication, CBT, and IPT	Chapter 1
5	Evidence for the Effectiveness of Guided Self-Help	Review of the evidence for the effectiveness of supervised self-help for both BN and BED	Chapter 1
6	An Assessment of Your Eating Problems: Is it Time to Begin Treatment?	Determining readiness for treatment	Chapter 3
7	Understanding and Applying the CBT Model	Application of the CBT model of binge eating and purging to the patient	Chapter 4
8	Using Daily Food Records to Monitor Eating	Description of Daily Food Records and how to use them	Chapter 4
9	Establishing a Regular Pattern of Eating plus Weekly Weighing	Introduction of eating by the clock (three meals and two snacks per day at regular intervals)	Chapter 4
10	Feared and Problem Foods	Identification of "bad" or "off limits" foods and how to incorporate them into the patient's daily diet	Chapter 11
11	Body-Image Concerns	How to eliminate body checking behaviors	Chapter 12
12	Handling Intense Moods and Emotions	Ways of dealing with intense mood states	Chapter 14
13	Working Through Problem Situations and Thoughts	Introduction of problem-solving method and cognitive restructuring technique	Chapter 13
14	Handling Challenging People	Exploration of personal relationships; dealing with "coaches" and "saboteurs"	Chapter 14
15	Preventing Relapse and Maintaining Change	Handling lapses, preventing relapse, and maintaining positive changes	Chapter 15

change her behavior between sessions based on what she reads in the workbook. Point out that all subsequent sessions will be 25 minutes long and that it is important for the patient to be on time for each one.

- Give the patient a copy of the workbook. Encourage the patient to underline anything she doesn't understand so you can discuss any questions at the next session. Instruct the patient to use the Daily Food Records for the next week.

- Discuss with the patient what she hopes to achieve in treatment. If issues about weight arise, refer the patient to chapter 9 of the workbook and reassure her that most patients do not gain weight during treatment. In fact, overweight patients tend to lose weight once they establish a regular pattern of eating and their binge eating diminishes.

- Schedule the next session and all remaining sessions, if possible.

Session 2 Outline

- Greet the patient, remind her that this is Session 2, and confirm how many sessions are left.

- Ask how the patient is doing to get a general picture of her progress in reading the book and examining her readiness to change.

- Ask the patient if she has any questions about what she read. If the answer is in the workbook, refer the patient to the particular chapter and page.

- Review two or three pages of the patient's completed Daily Food Records and ask her to point out bad and good days. This review should focus on the timing of meals and on progress (if any) toward regular eating (three meals and two snacks each day). Reiterate the rationale for establishing a regular eating pattern.

- Assign homework and confirm the time of the next session. Instruct the patient to continue reading chapters 1–6 of the workbook, and also chapter 8, which discusses establishing a regular eating pattern.

Outline for Subsequent Sessions

The preparation for subsequent sessions is the same as for the first two sessions; the format of subsequent sessions follows.

- Greet the patient and remind her of the session number and how many sessions or weeks are left.

- Ask how the patient is doing to ascertain her progress.

- Check on the homework and ask the patient if she has any questions about the material presented in the workbook. Again, refer the patient to the particular chapter(s) and page(s).

- Briefly review the patient's completed Daily Food Records, focusing on the current work but also looking at her success with other program recommendations (e.g., regularizing her eating patterns).

- Summarize the patient's progress and assign homework, which may or may not include moving on to the next step of treatment.

- Confirm the time of the next session.

Treatment Considerations

The therapist should be familiar with Chapter 2 of this guide, which discusses special considerations for bulimia nervosa and binge-eating disorder. In particular, review the section on other forms of purging and how to deal with them.

Compliance Problems

Promptly address any problems the patient is having adhering to the program. See Chapter 7 of this guide for types of compliance problems and suggestions for addressing them.

Focus of Therapy

Because the treatment sessions are short, it is extremely important to focus treatment on the problematic eating. There is no time to examine other life problems.

References

Agras, W. S., Crow, S. J., Halmi, K. A., Mitchell, J. E., Wilson, G. T., & Kraemer, H. C. (2000). Outcome predictors for the cognitive-behavioral treatment of bulimia nervosa: Data from a multisite study. *American Journal of Psychiatry, 157,* 1302–1308.

Agras, W. S., Rossiter, E. M., Arnow, B., Schneider, J. A., Telch, C. F., Raeburn, S. D., et al. (1992). Pharmacologic and cognitive-behavioral treatment for bulimia nervosa: A controlled comparison. *American Journal of Psychiatry, 149*(1), 82–87.

Agras, W. S., Rossiter, E. M., Arnow, B., Telch, C. F., Raeburn, S. D., Bruce, B., et al. (1994). One-year follow-up of psychosocial and pharmacologic treatments for bulimia nervosa. *Journal of Clinical Psychiatry, 55*(5), 179–183.

Agras, W. S., Telch, C. F., Arnow, B., Eldredge, K., & Marnell, M. (1997). One-year follow-up of cognitive-behavioral therapy for obese individuals with binge eating disorder. *Journal of Consulting and Clinical Psychology, 65*(2), 343–347.

Agras, W. S., Telch, C. F., Arnow, B., Eldredge, K., Wilfley, D. E., Raeburn, S. D., et al. (1994). Weight loss, cognitive-behavioral, and desipramine treatments in binge eating disorder: An additive design. *Behavior Therapy, 25,* 209–238.

Agras, W. S., Walsh, B. T., Fairburn, C. G., Wilson, G. T., & Kraemer, H. C. (2000). A multicenter comparison of cognitive-behavioral therapy and interpersonal psychotherapy for bulimia nervosa. *Archives of General Psychiatry, 57,* 459–466.

Banasiak, S. J., Paxton, S. J., & Hay, P. (2005). Guided self-help for bulimia nervosa in primary care: A randomized controlled trial. *Psychological Medicine, 35,* 1283–1294.

Barlow, D.H. (2004). Psychological treatments. *American Psychologist, 59,* 869–878.

Fairburn, C. G., Norman, P. A., Welch, S. L., O'Connor, M. E., Doll, H. A., & Peveler, R. C. (1995). A prospective study of outcome in bulimia nervosa and the long-term effects of three psychological treatments. *Archives of General Psychiatry, 52*(4), 304–312.

Fluoxetine Bulimia Nervosa Study Group (1992). Fluoxetine in the treatment of bulimia nervosa. *Archives of General Psychiatry, 49,* 139–147.

Goldbloom, D. S., Olmsted, M., Davis, R., Clewes, J., Heinmaa, M., Rockert, W., et al. (1997). A randomized controlled trial of fluoxetine and cognitive-behavioral therapy for bulimia nervosa: Short-term outcome. *Behavior Research & Therapy, 35,* 803–811.

Grilo, C. M., & Masheb, R. M. (2005). A randomized controlled trial of guided self-help cognitive behavioral therapy and behavioral weight loss for binge eating disorder. *Behavior Research & Therapy, 43,* 1509–1525,

Grilo, C. M., Masheb, R. M., & Salant, S. L. (2005). Cognitive behavioral therapy guided self-help and orlistat for the treatment of binge eating disorder: A randomized, double-blind, placebo-controlled trial. *Biological Psychiatry, 57,* 1193–1201.

Grilo, C. M., Masheb, R. M., & Wilson, G. T. (2005). Efficacy of cognitive behavioral therapy and fluoxetine for the treatment of binge eating disorder: A randomized double-blind placebo-controlled comparison. *Biological Psychiatry, 57,* 301–309.

Grilo, C. M., Masheb, R. M., & Wilson, G. T. (2006). Rapid response to treatment for binge eating disorder. *Journal of Consulting and Clinical Psychology, 74,* 602–613.

Hsu, L. K., Clement, L., Santhouse, R., & Ju, E. S. (1991). Treatment of bulimia nervosa with lithium carbonate: A controlled study. *Journal of Nerve and Mental Disorders, 179*(6), 351–355.

Hudson, J. I., McElroy, S. L., Raymond, N. C., Crow, S., Keck, P. E., Jr., Carter, W. P., et al. (1998). Fluvoxamine in the treatment of binge-eating disorder: A multicenter placebo-controlled, double-blind trial. *American Journal of Psychiatry, 155*(12), 1756–1762.

Institute of Medicine. (2001). Crossing the quality chasm: A new health system for the 21st century. Washington, DC: National Academy Press.

Mitchell, J. E., Fletcher, L., Hanson, K., et al., (2001). The relative efficacy of fluoxetine and manual-based self-help in the treatment of outpatients with bulimia nervosa. *Journal of Clinical Psychopharmacy, 21*(21), 298–304.

Mitchell, J. E., Hoberman, H. N., Peterson, C. B., Mussell, M., & Pyle, R. L. (1996). Research on the psychotherapy of bulimia nervosa: Half empty or half full. *International Journal of Eating Disorders, 20*(3), 219–229.

Mitchell, J. E., Pyle, R. L., Eckert, E. D., Hatsukami, D., Pomeroy, C., & Zimmerman, R. (1990). A comparison study of antidepressants and structured intensive group psychotherapy in the treatment of bulimia nervosa. *Archives of General Psychiatry, 47,* 149–157.

Newman-Toker, J. (2000). Risperidone in anorexia nervosa. *Journal of the American Academy of Child & Adolescent Psychiatry, 39,* 941–942.

Palmer, R. L., Birchall, H., McGrain, L., & Sullivan, V. Self-help for bulimic disorders: A randomised controlled trial comparing minimal guidance with face-to-face or telephone guidance (2002). *British Journal of Psychiatry, 181,* 230–235.

Pope, H. G., Hudson, J. I., & Jonas, J. M. (1985). Antidepressant treatment of bulimia: A two-year follow-up study. *Journal of Clinical Psychopharmacy, 5,* 254–259.

Pope, H. G., Hudson, J. I., Jonas, J. M., & Yurgelin-Todd, D. (1983). Bulimia treated with impramine: A placebo-controlled, double-blind study. *American Journal of Psychiatry, 140,* 554–558.

Pope, H. G., Keck, P. E., & McElroy, S. L. (1989). A placebo-controlled study of trazadone in bulimia nervosa. *Journal of Clinical Psychopharmacy, 9,* 254–259.

Shah, N., Passi, V., Bryson, S., & Agras, W. S. (2005). Patterns of eating and abstinence in women treated for bulimia nervosa. *International Journal of Eating Disorders, 38,* 330–334.

Telch, C. F., Agras, W. S., Rossiter, E. M., Wilfley, D., & Kenardy, J. (1990). Group cognitive-behavioral treatment for the non-purging bulimic: An initial evaluation. *Journal of Consulting and Clinical Psychology, 58,* 629–635.

Telch, C. F., & Stice, E. (1998). Psychiatric comorbidity in women with binge eating disorder: Prevalence rates from a non-treatment-seeking sample. *Journal of Consulting and Clinical Psychology, 66*(5), 768–776.

Walsh, B. T., Agras, W. S., Devlin, M. J., Fairburn, C. G., Wilson, G. T., Kahn, C., et al. (2000). Fluoxetine for bulimia nervosa following poor response to psychotherapy. *American Journal of Psychiatry, 157*(8), 1332–1334.

Walsh, B. T., Gladis, M., & Roose, S. P. (1988). Phenelzine vs. placebo in 50 patients with bulimia. *Archives of General Psychiatry, 45,* 471–475.

Walsh, B. T., Stewart, J. W., & Roose, S. P. (1984). Treatment of bulimia with monoamine oxidase inhibitors. *American Journal of Psychiatry, 139,* 1629–1630.

Walsh, B. T., Wilson, G. T., Loeb, K. L., Devlin, M. J., Pike, K. M., Roose, et al. (1997). Medication and psychotherapy in the treatment of bulimia nervosa. *American Journal of Psychiatry, 154*(4), 523–531.

Wilfley, D. E., Welch, R. R., Stein, R. I., Spurrell, E. B., et al. (2002). A randomized comparison of group cognitive-behavioral therapy and group interpersonal therapy for the treatment of overweight individuals with binge eating disorder. *Archives of General Psychiatry, 59*, 713–721.

Wiser, S., & Telch, C. F. (1999). Dialectical behavior therapy for binge-eating disorder. *Journal of Clinical Psychology, 55*(6), 755–768.

Yanovski, S. Z., Nelson, J. E., & Dubbert, B. K. (1992). Association of binge-eating disorder and psychiatric comorbidity in the obese. *American Journal of Psychiatry, 150*, 1472–1479.

About the Authors

W. Stewart Agras earned his medical degree from University College, London, England, in 1955 and then completed his residency and fellowship at McGill University, Montreal, Canada. He was an early leader in the field of behavior therapy. At the University of Vermont, he became interested in phobia as a model for psychotherapy research, and, in collaboration with Harold Leitenberg, PhD, discovered that exposure to the feared situation was a principal ingredient of treatment for phobias. After moving to the University of Mississippi Medical Center as chairman of the Department of Psychiatry in 1969, he established the department as an active research center focused on behavioral psychotherapy, establishing the psychology residency program with David Barlow. In 1973, he moved to Stanford University as a professor of psychiatry, establishing one of the first behavioral-medicine programs in the country, and becoming the first and founding president of the Society for Behavioral Medicine. When the upsurge in patients with bulimia nervosa occurred in the late '70s, he began research into the etiology and treatment of the disorder, conducting a number of important treatment trials for bulimia nervosa, together with the first treatment studies for binge-eating disorder. In addition, he has been president of the Association for the Advancement of Behavior Therapy and editor of the *Journal of Applied Behavior Analysis and the Annals of Behavioral Medicine,* and has twice been a fellow at the Center for Advanced Studies in the Behavioral Sciences.

Robin F. Apple received her PhD from the University of California–Los Angeles in 1991 and has published articles and chapters in the area of eating disorders. She has also cowritten a patient manual and a therapist guide that use cognitive-behavioral therapy to help patients prepare for weight-loss surgery. In her current role as associate clinical professor, Department of Psychiatry and Behavioral Sciences, Stanford University, she has an active role training postdoctoral psychology fellows and psychiatry residents to use CBT and other treatment techniques, and has provided short- and long-term individual therapy and group therapy for those dealing with eating disorders and a range of other issues. Dr. Apple also maintains a varied caseload in her private practice in Palo Alto, California, and she is a consultant with the county medical center's eating-disorders program, a contributor to a multi-center weight-loss surgery research study, and has been an expert witness in forensics related to weight-loss surgery.